Go to Grow

Why every believer would benefit from participating on a short term mission

David McDougall

Onwards and Upwards Publishers

Berkeley House, 11 Nightingale Crescent, Leatherhead, Surrey, KT24 6PD.

www.onwardsandupwards.org

ISBN:	**978-1-907509-60-5**
Illustrations:	**Amanda Pollard**
Cover photograph:	**Dylan Walters**
Cover design:	**Guilherme Gustavo Condeixa**

Printed in the UK

For Kim, Nicol, Jamie and Arran

who have supported and joined
me as I have been invited to visit
many places around God's
amazing world.

Endorsements

David McDougall thinks globally and has inspired many on short-term mission visits with long-term benefits locally. David has discovered a way to infuse faith, hope and love in people.

Revd Canon J John

David McDougall has a great track record in taking people away on mission - all kinds of people, not just the extrovert and obviously gifted ones. I've witnessed at first hand the impact of these mission trips, not least in the lives of the missioners themselves and the churches from which they've come. David's book is both inspiring and practical. His vision, and mine, is that many more churches might catch the vision of sending people on mission, in obedience to Jesus' call, both to be disciples and to make disciples.

The Rt Revd Andrew Watson,
Bishop of Aston

We go on mission trips not simply to try and change the world, but knowing that God will change us. This book is a wonderful exploration of the journeys that many take when they get involved with short-term missions and the fruit of that experience. It's full of challenging and inspiring stories of lives transformed and offers great practical application. I hope it will inspire many more churches to get involved.

Sarah Wigglesworth
Transform Team Leader
Tearfund

Contents

Foreword by Ben Jeffery

When was the first time you discovered poverty? I remember as a teenager watching Comic Relief and seeing poverty in its most aggressive and shocking form on the TV in my lounge and thinking, "Someone has to do something about this." I remember feeling frustrated that actors and musicians who earned millions of pounds each year were asking me, a poor student, for money. I thought that *they* should give away their fortunes and make a difference, instead of asking *me* to give from the little I had.

So I did nothing.

A few years later I began to understand more about politics, and I learnt for the first time how much money we had spent on wars, armies and national defence. I was appalled, and I remember thinking to myself, "There are starving children in Africa and our government is spending billions on weapons and death." I fumed and vented my outrage to my friends who all agreed with me that this was not right or fair.

But we did nothing.

I don't think that anyone has ever had to convince me that mission is important. The need has always been obvious. The writer William Hazlitt once wrote, "Man is the only animal that laughs and weeps; for he is the only animal that is struck with the difference between what things are and what they ought to be." Likewise, I have always known that it isn't fair that some people live in luxury and wealth while others struggle for basic food and water. It isn't fair that some people are born into Christian families while there are still so many that are born into communities where they will never hear the name of Jesus. However, it always felt like something so remote and far away, something that was someone else's responsibility to fix.

So I did nothing.

Reading David McDougall's book, I was quick to notice that for him mission is not something distant. It is not something that is for other people to get involved with but an integral part of God's plan for each and every one of us to engage with. He looks at a broken world, missing God's love and asks, "*What can I do* to help you fix this Lord?"

Every journey starts with a single step, and every step starts with a decision. In a world of distractions, stresses and bright lights it is easy for mission to get lost or safely tucked away in the 'think about this later' part of our brains. For some people they feel too young; others feel too old. Some have a career they are nurturing, and others have a family to worry about. So we all too easily find ourselves ten years down the line with nothing changed and nothing done. David boldly takes the first step of this journey for us and shows us step by step what mission is, what it involves and what will happen to us. He has clearly lived what he has written and his incredible stories lead us forward into exploring mission and opening our eyes to what God is doing – and what He wants to do in us too.

Having served as an Anglican minister for a quarter of a century and having taken hundreds of people on mission trips, David has an immense wealth of experience. In 'Go to Grow' he does not to shirk from the challenges and the cost of mission but faces them head on and comes out triumphantly looking for the next hurdle to overcome and opportunity to serve. He recognises that we all have something to give, that we all have a difference that we can make and that there is a world desperate for help. While acknowledging the personal sacrifices involved and the benefits for others, he looks at the big picture and realises that there is a simple truth for each person that engages in mission; whether we are reaching out to teenagers on a difficult estate or travelling to the slums of Mumbai to give children an education and hope for the future, we always grow when we go.

You may have noticed the transformation in the faces of people that you have known to have gone on mission teams for the first time and returned home. It is incredible hearing about the work that they have done and the lives they have helped in some way. More incredible still is the way that they seem to have grown and changed. For me this is as impacting as anything else they have achieved.

This reaction that takes places in us has instilled in David a passion which resonates and radiates from the pages of this book. It is to see people partner with God in seeing the lost found, the broken made whole and the hurt comforted. It is a passion that drives people to the ends of the Earth with the gospel and which cries out from the hearts of people working in desperate situations around the world today. It is a passion that will see the church in the UK and around the world enriched and blessed through service in mission. It is a passion that echoes God's desire to pour out His love on the nations.

My personal journey in mission did not end with me hoping that someone else would go and do something about it. One day, I decided to step up and go to Rwanda, becoming part of a team working with genocide victims and the local church in Kigali. I took the step to go and see how God wanted to use me, and now I have the privilege of taking people from around the UK on similar journeys.

As you read this book you will be faced with the same questions that David was faced with on his trips. Is your life safe, comfortable and cosy? What would you do to be part of God's plan to fix this broken world? Using this book as an experienced guide to help you to explore, learn and grapple with the challenge of mission, you may find yourself engaging in a journey you have never dreamed of before.

My prayer for you is that this book will become the beginning of an incredible adventure in your life. I pray that God will challenge you, that He will use you, that you will be a blessing to others and that God will cause you to grow too. It won't be safe, comfortable and cosy, but it will be worth it.

Ben Jeffery
Missions Motivator
Interserve

Introduction

Aberdovey on the coast of Wales is a stunning place to begin to write this book, and being away from home reminds me of the commonly agreed principle that being away from home for work or rest creates the longing to be back again with fresh enthusiasm. It's good to be away and it's wonderful to get back home!

All through my twenty five years as an Anglican minister I have taken hundreds of different people away from home on short-term visits, both to places in the United Kingdom or abroad. I have noticed that on the return of my team members to their various churches there have been major effects on their attitude to and involvement with their local church. It has made a profound difference to their life and witness generally, and I have come to the conclusion that these visits are a profoundly effective tool in the process of discipleship. I have, as importantly, noticed that these visits leave team members with an increased motivation for mission that can be seen in them personally and then expressed through their local church.

I acknowledge right at the start of this book that the biggest benefit of any short-term mission activity must most importantly be experienced by the situations we are invited to go to. No team I have ever led has been self-invited; all my teams have had the received location in mind first, and it has never been my intention to create visits in order only to bless the lives of team members. However, through the many teams I have taken away it is very noticeable and wonderful that team members' lives have been transformed. Whilst much is written about the fruitfulness of mission in the context of the receiving situation, not much at all has been written on the benefits to the Christian or their local churches of going on such faith adventures. This is why I have decided to write some of these fruits down and spend some time reflecting on them.

I have been asked twice to write a book on personal discipleship and have been so busy as an evangelist and minister that I have not been able to write one. However, now I have the time to write I find myself answering that request but from perhaps a slightly different perspective. Short-term mission visits are an incredibly valuable way of creating deeply disciplined disciples of Jesus Christ, and because of these visits mission becomes a much higher priority in the churches these people belong to. There is contagiousness and passion which people come back with, that fires other people up around them. As a church leader this is so incredibly helpful; people with passion and excitement about their faith create the likelihood of hot, fiery, mission-focused parish life – and that's what we need in England today.

This summer, twenty-five of my church family from St Saviour's Church, Sunbury, will join me on a very practical mission visit to Gulu in Uganda. The team will be building a classroom in a Watoto[1] Village. These communities are formed for the many HIV/AIDS orphans of that nation, and there they have homes, parents, education, medical care and spiritual nurture. Gary and Marilyn Skinner, who are the founders of Watoto Uganda, are amazing servants of God and have brought hope to thousands of orphan children and abused women in Uganda. Part of the team will be working alongside the Living Hope project, which is rescuing women from the bush who have been abandoned and maimed by Joseph Coney's ruthless regime, The Lord's Resistance Army. It is very possible for you to join a 'Global Team' through the Visit Africa programme run by the UK Watoto office in Dagenham. Contact details can be found in the back of this book.

Why are so many coming with me this year? Because so many have gone in the previous nine years and have come back fired up and longing to make a difference in this dark world in which we live. When we engage in a personal way with situations that desperately need the love of God shown, we come alive spiritually. If, on the other hand, we just reach into our pocket and give money to an organisation to do the work with no personal involvement, it doesn't take long before the giving subsides. Personal involvement, understanding and prayer are keys to Christians remaining involved in mission both at home and abroad.

The teams that I have taken away have always been a total mixture of people from all kinds of backgrounds. I remember telling one church

---

[1] Watoto is based in Uganda, founded by Pastor Gray and Marilyn Skinner

leader that I was taking away a particular member of their congregation and they could not believe it – they felt the risk was immense! On that mission that individual shone like they had never done in the local church and God used them immensely in that situation. It has had a profound effect on their life and ministry since. These visits I am talking about are not only for the 'professional Christians', but for all church members.

I have received the following type of invitations at home or abroad, where I have invited people to join me on a team:

- UK University Missions
- Town-wide Missions - Springboard
- Church Weekends Away
- Alpha Events
- Living Water Events – East Anglia
- Soul Survivor Events
- New Wine Events
- Watoto Missions
- SOMA (Sharing of Ministry Abroad) Missions to Congo, Tanzania and Uganda
- Missions where I have been given personal invitations - such as to South Africa, Ukraine, Russia, Former Yugoslavia and many times to Uganda

Many of the stories I will use in this particular book come from experiences with SOMA, who have encouraged me to lead teams, especially to Africa. I want to commend their work as an Anglican short-term mission agency that does an incredible work in many parts of the world, bringing hope in Jesus and spiritual renewal.

I will begin each chapter with a real-life experience story from a short-term mission visit and then explain its impact both on the person and on the local church.

There are so many advantages of such short-term mission visits - here are a few of them:

- It gives the opportunity to respond to God's command to go to all nations and is a practical application of the Great Commission
- It brings maturity of faith by stepping out into what are often very uncomfortable situations
- It helps the believer to realise what God's worldwide church looks like and thereby expands the world-view of the believer
- In all kinds of ways it can encourage those who are long-term missionaries, who can often feel forgotten or lonely or remote from their supporting churches
- It enables Christians to understand the culture, challenges and opportunities the missionaries they are supporting are involved with on a daily basis
- It enables missionaries' supporters to be able to pray more personally, specifically and therefore effectively
- It enables the Christian to learn more about cultures different to their own and what it means to continue believing in that situation
- It heightens the awareness and need for mission, both in the team member and, on return, to their local church
- It can inspire team members to become full-time workers on the mission field
- It gives the opportunity to share your faith personally in ways that perhaps you never have and this, in turn, helps you to share your faith more readily when you return home
- Team members often find they are ministered to more deeply than they minister, learning to receive as well as give
- It helps us to realise that we can make a difference in people's lives.
- So many recipients of teams in many countries (especially places like the Congo) have said that it's as powerful for us purely to stand alongside them as it is for us to bring them help.
- The experience has often had a long-term impact on the team members' lives; for some, 'money' has never been looked at in the same way

- Team members find areas of gifting on these visits that they never realised they had!
- Many who have travelled with me have said that it was only on these mission visits that they realised how well fed they were spiritually and how what they knew came to memory when they got sharing; but, even more wonderfully, that what they knew came alive more in them once it had been shared instead of just stored.

Of course there are real dangers - here are some:

- Cultural insensitivity
- Too heavy a burden on long term missionaries
- Culture shock and reverse culture shock on return to home
- Lack of preparation of programme, communication or health protection
- Lack of training in how to speak through an interpreter
- Guilt can be an issue where westerners can be overwhelmed by their wealth in the face of poverty
- People going it alone, rather than with an umbrella organisation, e.g. SOMA or Watoto

However, faced with the huge number of advantages that I shall more deeply explore, I do believe that it is very worthwhile for as many as possible to join a short-term mission adventure at some point in their Christian life.

In the following pages I want to map out some of the many fruits that short-term visits have created in people's lives and in doing so hope to encourage you and others to join a team soon. You will never regret it!

1

Lose Two Thirds of Your Luggage

Sacrifice/Choices/Giving/Materialism

We had just completed a wonderful visit in Karamoja in North Uganda and were waiting for the MAF flight (Mission Aviation Fellowship) that was going to pick us up from an airfield that was no more than a long uneven field with one hut!

After quite a long wait I told the team to listen, as in the distance I could hear the *high-pitched* mosquito-like sound of the plane coming our way. The excitement of going home was immense – much as we had enjoyed all that God had been doing in that situation, we were very much looking forward to returning home.

The plane landed. The MAF pilot took one look at our team and the pile of luggage and proclaimed, "You all need to lose two thirds of your luggage!" He then explained to me that the plane would not actually take off with the full weight of the team and all their bags. On the previous inbound journey a bigger plane had been used, but no one had told this pilot what the needs were and so he had arrived with a smaller plane.

As I explained to the team that our choices were either to wait a day or two for a different plane with added costs attached or lose two thirds of our luggage, you can imagine the reaction! However, the team wanted to get back to Kampala to catch their BA flight home the next day for all sorts of different reasons - not least the fact that several needed to get back to their workplaces. Therefore everyone began the task of choosing what they would keep and what they would give away!

The villagers and clergy that we had been working with looked on with great excitement as the pile that would be left behind for them grew steadily higher. Things put on that growing mound were of all kinds, such as laptops, Bibles, books, clothes, speaking notes, medicines, toiletries and shoes.

The pilot, on weighing the load, told us once again that more had to go! So, more precious possessions were added to the pile. Gifts given by the villagers were kept, as valuable personal items were given away; it was sacrificial and turned out to be a deep life experience that over the years has become a much-repeated story.

Eventually the pilot was happy and so were the locals! We just about took off and headed for home via Kampala! Even as we journeyed we experienced a growing sense of freedom and joy, having given so much away. Jesus said:

Luke 6:38
Give and it will be given to you. A good measure, pressed down, shaken together and running over, will be poured into your lap.

This scripture became real to us not in material terms but in deep spiritual joy. We had not sought this; we had not found it easy; but we were beginning to realise its freedom on that flight and have increasingly ever since that time, as we have continued to learn the joy of giving.

For many years now the members of that particular team have recounted this experience. It was for all of us one of those times when God taught us some deep life lessons that touched especially on what is really valuable, true sacrifice, our belongings and especially about giving.

Giving away two thirds of what we had was a really difficult thing to do. None of us really wanted to do it, but we had little choice. As we went through our stuff it was a real problem deciding what was going to be kept and what we were to give away. I remember giving away a Bible that I had treasured for many years – one that had many little notes, references, quotes, short talks and had been given to me by my parents. But it was just too heavy and there were other things that I wanted to keep.

It was also interesting to me that for some of those team members giving away a third was not at all a problem. They set to and gave away from their belongings quickly and without fuss. This aspect of discipleship had already been learnt by them, but for the rest of us we were still learning.

The experience here was teaching us about all kinds of things:

- Our personal reactions to such a request
- Our attitude to our belongings
- Our ability to give away

Jesus said:

Acts 20:35
It is more blessed to give than to receive.

In fact, the Bible generally teaches us that we find by losing, we are raised by being humbled and, as here in Acts, we receive by giving away. At the time we were not aware of, or even that happy about, the challenge that we faced. On reflection, and ever since, this simple but profound challenge has changed us.

Many years ago I was taught brilliantly by Rev Martin Peppiatt that truly blessed people are not those who are looking for a window of heaven to be opened above themselves; rather they are people who are willing to be themselves, allowing God to use them as an open window for His blessings to be poured out on others. During that visit God had been opening the windows of our lives as a team and pouring out through us what He wanted. Now, even in the last moments in Karamoja, he was still doing it but this time in a physical form – giving away material things!

In the local church we have a big issue with Christians in terms of their giving. People just do not see the joy of it and give from what's left over, rather than from their main portion. Many churches' finances are crippled because of this and their work frustrated. We have to run stewardship campaigns to balance our budgets and continuously work hard to raise money for projects. It really should not be like this; there should be enough amongst God's local people to do the work of God in that area and away from it.

When I was Associate Vicar of St Stephen's Twickenham we learned that the more we gave away in terms of people or resources, the more God gave back. The first time we church-planted in 2000 our then vicar, Andrew Watson, was particularly worried about the loss of income but also the loss of people. It took only five months until we were numerically and financially stronger than before we had planted. Exactly the same happened again when the church plant I took from there happened in 2002! Give and it will be given to you in abundance!

One test of discipleship is to examine our bank account and see if it reveals us as a Christian or not. Does it state your commitment to God's work locally and away? Is giving a priority, or is it provision given from the margins?

Another test of how deep our discipleship is, is to go through our homes and see if our lifestyle reflects sacrifice or personal comfort. I am not saying our homes should not be wonderful places, but I am challenging overindulgence. Why do we need new furniture so often, the kitchen replaced before it's worn out and a new car rather than one a few years old? Why do we have too many clothes and crazy amounts of pairs of shoes? Why are there so many suits never worn or dresses rarely seen?

Why are there so many toys, that we end up car-booting them for little or, even worse, just throwing them away?

The trouble is we live in a part of the world where there is just too much of everything and sometimes, without realising it, we get caught up in that lifestyle. We end up not valuing what we have got and just seeking the short-lived thrill of buying the next new commodity that we think will make us happy.

When children are chasing your jeep just so you might throw them a sweet or toy or pencil, you realise how little they have. When you play football with African kids who are playing with a stick bound by cloth to make a ball, you realise that you have been so fortunate to have had amazing footballs to play with. When you stand alongside people who are naked or people living in ripped rags for clothing, your attitude to clothing changes. When you meet people who live on a dollar a week, you are severely challenged about your enormous earnings. These are some of the vital lessons to be learnt by being involved abroad, and so our discipleship deepens.

Final thought: Many years ago I remember being challenged by a preacher to live more 'lightly' by going through the house and giving as much away as possible. Kim and I set to it, de-cluttering as much as possible – it was liberating. What we could give to people we did, what we could give to charity shops we gave, and what just needed dumping we chucked. The end result was a wonderful sense of freedom. In the West we live with too much; we fill our lives with too many things and they slow us down.

Action:

1. Take a walk around your house and garage and think what could be given away.

2. Write down a list of ten things from your house that you could give away.

    1)

    2)

    3)

    4)

    5)

    6)

    7)

    8)

    9)

    10)

3. Discuss with a friend how you would have reacted to giving away two thirds of what you had.

4. Discuss together what you would have given away and what you would have kept.

5. Discuss together whether you would you have stayed a few days longer and incurred the extra cost.

6. Discuss together what has taught you along the way to live lightly and give sacrificially.

2

Surrounded by Warriors

Trust/Dependence on God/Unity/Contentment

We had just arrived in another tiny African field airport and, as we landed, the MAF pilot alerted my attention to the fact that Masai Warriors were waiting for us! As the plane came to a stop, these tall, tribal warriors surrounded the aircraft.

It was a surreal moment. It was very quiet. The pilot told me that usually when this happened they were looking for medical supplies and that we were in no particular danger – the team were not so convinced!

The pilot was very calm and gave the warriors what he felt that they were wanting from the plane, but things seemed to reach an impasse. The pilot distracted their attention enough for me to leave the team in his hands and to wander off into the bush, heading for the road I had spotted on the descent. Usually I would never do anything alone, but on this occasion there seemed little choice and I pretended I needed the toilet!

On the descent I had seen the local road winding to the nearest town, and I had decided that if we got into real trouble that would be my best means of reaching someone to help us.

I set off in search of the road I had spotted. Not long after finding it, a four-by-four vehicle came along and amazingly gave me a lift into the next town. The driver informed me of some Canadian aid workers living there who might help us out of this situation. God answers prayer! Amazingly I located the aid workers, told them what was happening and they immediately came out with me and helped us out of a tricky situation. All was settled peacefully, and the MAF pilot was pleased to leave us to get back to his base!

The team and I had much to praise God for, and we all learned a great deal through this experience. One of our greatest lessons learnt was to trust in God when things seem impossible. It really did feel dangerous; none of us were sure what would happen and we had to put our trust fully in God and in leaders. This was expressed by trusting leadership, praying quietly but fervently, remaining calm and sticking together.

Trusting leadership, fervent prayer, staying calm and remaining loyal to one another are attributes desperately needed in both the mature Christian and in the local church, if it's going to be growing and healthy. So often these characteristics are missing for many reasons, but rather than bemoan that they are not there, we can do something positive to restore them; what I am suggesting is just one way of doing so. Every minister longs for their people to trust them, for the people to be passionately prayerful and for unity to be an increasing reality.

So much of our lives is spent in safety that we can learn a great deal by stepping out of our comfort zones. Dependence on God is a strong basis of daily discipleship. In the West we find it difficult to learn this vital aspect because life is relatively safe and easy. I have found that in much of Africa life is very different indeed and that, to survive, Africans learn to become totally dependent on God for all of life.

The Rev Ian Pusey, my brilliant training vicar, often used a phrase that has really stayed with me:

Jesus came to comfort the disturbed and to disturb the comfortable.

By leaving your home, your church and your immediate friendship group for a short-term mission visit, you will experience what it is to be disturbed from your comfortable Western lifestyle. This will allow you the opportunity to rely on God like you have perhaps never done before.

I have learnt so much from African Christians. The two greatest lessons have come in two areas that are deeply rooted in African discipleship:

- Dependence on God
- Godly contentment

For daily provision and health, African Christians depend wholly on God and then, in seeing how He provides for them, they live contented lives. This contentment is not shallow; it is very deep and is one of the reasons for the incredible joy and happiness found in their lives. These two aspects have had a profound effect on my life, and I will always be so grateful to them for these aspects that I have learnt from them. Talking to some Africans in England recently made me realise once again that these two lessons of dependence on God and godly contentment are two of the greatest lessons the Western world needs to learn from the African Christian. If we were to fully live these two foundational discipleship lessons, our lives as Christians and our local churches would be very different indeed.

My team put their trust in God, and throughout that visit – which was once again an extraordinary time of heaven touching earth – the team learned as much at the start of it via these tribal warriors' welcome as they did through the Holy Spirit gatherings that followed.

Jesus said:

Mark 12:30
Love the Lord your God with all your heart and with all your soul and with all your mind and with all your strength.

Loving God means to deeply trust Him.

In recent years the lines of an old hymn often come to mind: "It is well, it is well with my soul." As I journey on, there is an increasing trust in God as leader of my life and that deepening trust brings a deep peace. The more we learn to trust God, the better we cope with whatever life throws at us.

One of my life friends, Rev. Peter Law, taught me early on in ministry a vital discipleship truth. "Acceptance is peace," Peter would often say. At first I thought it was strange and smacked of fatalism! The more I have reflected on it the more I realise its profound truth.

- Acceptance that God is fully in control of His creation, that He knows what is the very best for us even if what we are pleading for in prayer never comes.
- Acceptance that the end of our life stories will be good, even if the middle chapters seem a mixture of triumph and tragedy.
- Acceptance that we cannot humanly understand everything God does.

Acceptance is peace.

Often when teams have been away, things have happened very differently to what we would choose, have imagined or scheduled. As we accept what comes and work with it, so the peace of God flows in. Trying to manipulate things to be different, or just plain fighting against what God is unfolding, just creates frustration and failure. Those of us who like everything neatly packaged and programmes that run to exact plan should never come to Africa! There is a wonderful lady called Mary MacDonnell who has been on many SOMA teams over the years. One of her favourite sayings on such visits, when talking about the programs, is "It will emerge!" In other words, God will show us why we are really here in time, and then we must be light-footed enough to go with that rather than our ready-made, Western-style plans! "It will emerge" has become a kind of SOMA catchphrase over the years.

Much of the corruption one of my teams faced in the Congo (that I will talk about in a later chapter) was non-negotiable. We had to accept it many times over and so peace was restored. That's not to say I liked it or agreed with it, but it was a reality and it will take some time to change it. As in many areas of life we have to choose our battles.

Often we manage God out of what we are doing. We control things too tightly and as a result lose a great deal of fruitfulness and freedom.

Control is something many of us have problems with. Realising that God is in control comes slowly to most of us who, for whatever reason, try to control our own destinies. But when we begin to deeply trust God's control and his unfolding plan then we experience peace at a very deep level. Acceptance of God being in control is peace. It's God's world and it's God's church and we have the joy of loving Him.

If you have ever visited Africa you will know that any plans for a programme put together at home need to be lived with very lightly when you get to your invited destination. African time and African planning is something to be experienced! For English 'control freaks' it's the best way to learn to trust God. As we realise and allow God to be fully in control of our lives and activities, so our characters are enriched and there is more that God can pour out to others through the open window of our lives.

Getting out of your safety zone does not mean you have to come to Africa – it may mean stepping out and getting involved in fantastic projects that happen locally, such as Street Angels. This movement is growing in England, where local churches are getting onto the streets in some of the most troubled areas to reach out relationally to young people and make our communities safer and happier places in which to live. To do this takes courage, and by being involved in such projects or similar you can learn to trust God more deeply in this very comfortable part of God's world.

Action:

1. Write down three things that have taught you to become dependent on God.

    1)

    2)

    3)

2. In what ways does your life show godly contentment?

3. Discuss with a friend the statement "Acceptance is peace."

4. Discuss with a friend the following question: How dependent on God are we and does our culture work against this?

3

God's Protection

Provision/Protection/Prayer/Gifting/Control

Of all the places I have travelled to, DRC Congo is the most dangerous, troubled, destroyed, depressed and needy place. The human suffering that is going on there in these very days is terrible and is not talked about enough in our Western world. Every day people are disappearing, the rape of women is common and children are being forced by Joseph Coney into becoming 'child soldiers'. No one could have prepared me or the team fully for what we experienced on this visit!

The invitation was to Bukavu for a diocesan clergy conference and then some travelling in the local Anglican parishes. Our journey to Bukavu was not direct because one of the team, Rev Trevor Patterson, was keen for us to visit a missionary friend of his, Sarah Casson, who was working in Bunia. Flying to Bunia was straightforward; getting out of the airport without paying fictional fees was not! Eventually we went to visit Sarah and had an amazing time. In the period of that visit we were asked to bless her new home and learned huge amounts about the culture of DRC Congo.

I had been advised that, although the country had much unrest in certain areas, we were safe to travel and would be looked after en route. This was true and the colour purple often travelled with us in the front seat next to our driver!

At every airport in Congo we were met with huge difficulties, but by far the biggest one was the corruption of most airport staff and military personnel. I soon learned that the highest-ranking government officials were actively encouraging corruption at ground level so that people could have ways of earning money. We could not move unless we paid an exit fee or a yellow fever card-checking fee or an onward flight ticket confirmation fee. Everyone was after our dollars, and in a way I could quite understand it because people were desperately poor and in need of providing for their families.

As we began to travel around the country we could see the grand, old Dutch buildings of a bygone, wealthy era in terrible disrepair – a sign of a once thriving economy now in ruins. The people told us of the wonderful gorillas in the local forests; these would be visited by thousands if the tourist trade could be organised properly, but because there is no infrastructure at the moment nothing can be done. In any case, any tourist would not be able to stomach the daily barrage of corruption that they would be faced with. But one day, and I hope that it will not be too long, there will be a thriving tourist economy there that will bless the people and protect the incredible animals living in their jungles.

The team struggled in this situation. Delay after delay, charge after charge was made. Patience was severely stretched. In my training as a mission leader we were asked not to give in to such corruption, for fear that future teams would be increasingly caught by such charges. Yet in this situation there really was no choice; we could not move unless we paid up. The only possibility was a discount of what was being asked for, which for me, having been brought up in Bradford, North Yorkshire, came easily!

Eventually, after a twenty-four-hour delay in Bunia airport, we were allowed to fly internally but ended up with the plane being grounded at Beni in the middle of the jungle! Now what would happen and how would the team respond to this one?

Prayer had erupted on the plane, mainly because we were travelling with baggage and farming goods all around us and emergency signs were being held in place with sellotape! A strong sense of loyalty and a great deal of nervous laughter had begun to mark us out!

The team were so pleased when a miraculous God-incidence occurred through prayer – the Archbishop of Congo's son, John Paul, just so happened to be at Beni airport and swiftly took us to a beautiful Baptist guesthouse! We each had our own room, a meal was laid on for us and we were able to sleep.

None of that team will ever forget the incredible, internal journey we had through the Congo! As the team came to terms with the situation, we experienced all kinds of God-incidences and opportunities for sharing Jesus with people. One world banker we met was very much influenced by the team on a ferry journey across to Bukavu itself.

At the very start of the clergy conference the delegates were all informed that one of the vicars, on travelling to the event, had been abducted and was being held in the forests. Prayer exploded amongst those gathered and with our intercessors back at home. Within twenty four hours he had been released and joined the conference – to much celebration and joy.

Experiencing such things firsthand was huge for my team, and I know that it will always remain with them that prayer is powerful and that God does "watch over us" as Psalm 121 says. In fact this Psalm has been a rich source of assurance and help to many of my teams. The Psalmist is encouraging us to "lift our eyes to God" who is the source of help. He reminds us that God "neither slumbers nor sleeps" and therefore is protecting and providing for us all the time – we experienced this when we landed in the middle of the jungle and God's protection and provision was tangible!

My sister, Maggie Chan, came as a member of that team, and she humbly, nervously offered some health seminars each afternoon of the visit for the clergy and others attending the gathering. Maggie was being culturally sensitive; she did not want to offend by offering knowledge that they might already possess. So before we arrived she put together some HIV/AIDS, personal hygiene and basic health seminars. Maggie was sure in her own mind that she would give a brief seminar and that the attendees would not be open to asking questions publicly. So she was willing with a translator to do some one-to-one work after each session. How wrong could she be!

I remember that first session very well. Maggie got up and gave a twenty-minute introduction to general, personal health issues and then allowed a time of question and answers. Maggie was barraged for the next ninety minutes with a huge variety of questions, which she lovingly and patiently responded to. Never had she imagined the intense need for understanding of some of the most basic health issues. Every afternoon Maggie taught and then opened up a Q and A session, and I had quite a job to chair those meetings and try to bring them to a close! She became one of the most sought-after and respected members of the team.

It is so important to have a variety of differently-skilled people on any team, but to have a nurse travelling is a real bonus, not least for the health of the team itself but especially because they can invest much of their knowledge into the receiving situation. Maggie was a very busy lady that week! One of the most moving things Maggie had to respond to was when one of the team had a word of knowledge about 'machete wounds' that God would heal. Lots of people came forward for prayer, but there was one vicar that walked to the front, lifted his trousers and revealed the most terrible infected machete wound; he had been suffering with it for some time with no treatment. Over the week, through prayer and medical care, he went home a different person.

In the Congo we had to choose to put our trust in God. We knew we were going to an unsettled country, and we were as careful as we could be, always trying to make sure that someone travelled with us. It was dangerous and yet we were called to be there to stand alongside the local people. In the West we tend to forget – or even stop believing – that God protects us. We may fudge our beliefs by rationalising away basic tenets of the Christian faith because they seem so irrelevant to our situation. We slowly take control; it's as if we become God ourselves and have no need of the one true God. We protect ourselves, provide for ourselves and too often live without God at all. True Christianity is in real danger of extinction in the West and, as so often, the African Christians and their churches could well be our rescue.

At the end of an amazing time with the Bishop of Bukavu, his people and some from the town, we made our way sadly to the airport. It was a ten-mile journey on roads being built by the Chinese who, as usual in Africa, are plundering all the intensely valuable minerals to be found there. We passed many United Nations peacekeeping forces as we journeyed; they are very unpopular with the locals because they stand back and watch what happens without doing anything to help as daily abductions, rape and murder occur.

The journey was interspersed with stops for fictional travel charges of all kinds, but this time, because the well-known local bishop (in full purple) was travelling with us, we did not have to pay!

When we arrived at the airport there was no MAF assistant to greet us. This is rare because MAF and their staff are amazing and have never let me down. I was puzzled, as was the local bishop and his staff. Then we discovered why. The night before, there had been a raid in the local village and the militia had abducted and killed several people. One of these was a very close friend of the MAF assistant, and he had been comforting and helping the man's bereaved family. So, even as we left the soil of Congo, in our very last minutes, we were still hearing of terrible situations in that land.

Being in Congo is vital. I long to be there again soon, and I am only not there this year because elections in that land make the situation too dangerous to take teams in. They feel forgotten. They are in terrible trauma and in desperate need of us standing alongside them. We need to be there and make a difference to their lives.

Our short visit meant so much to the Congolese Christians, and they have been in much contact since that time. For my team it was a life-changing and challenging experience.

Action

1. Make a list of areas of expertise or experience you could offer to such a team.

   1)

   2)

   3)

   4)

   5)

2. Put aside thirty minutes to google what is happening in DRC Congo and then make a personal prayer list to work through.

   1)

   2)

   3)

   4)

   5)

4

I've Got Your Back

Encouragement/Empowering/Companionship
Accountability/Loyalty

Gail Foot, a good friend of mine, coined this phrase "I've got your back" and was using it when I took and her on a short-term visit to Donetsk in Ukraine. Since then I have adopted and treasured this team-building saying, which is terrific abroad but equally fruitful in the local church back at home.

Any public speaker will know that when you are in mid-flow and you can see in the people group in front of you an encouraging and supportive face beaming at you, things will go well! Gail has always done this for me, and when she is in the church or venue where I am speaking my confidence and anointing is higher. Whenever people do this for us as speakers we know they have "got our back" – in other words they are supporting us, willing us on, praying us through and loyal, whatever happens. It's such a spiritual richness to have that depth of discipleship on a team or in a church.

On the team in Donetsk we had all kinds of challenges to face, and the team Gail was on was a large one of about twenty people. As with every team the need for unity and pastoral care was essential. Gail taught the group how to do this by using this phrase but, more importantly, by modelling it brilliantly herself. She would come up to me just before I was about to speak to the patients of the sexually-transmitted disease clinic or in the terrifying prison there and say, "Dave, I've got your back." The releasing and empowering of this phrase, used and lived-out by a person you know, is incredible. If we could be this loving, this loyal and this empowering for each other in our local churches then anything could happen.

As a church-planting minister I have been in all kinds of tricky situations. Somehow Gail, or someone like her, has popped up just at the right time and given me the true sense of support and companionship that I needed in the tricky moment. Even just remembering that these people exist for me enables me to keep going when the road is very tough.

Jesus is recorded in Mark 2 as sending out his disciples in pairs. This was a deliberate action and, I am sure, intended to make sure that people did not 'go it alone'. We need each other, and we will be less likely to give up if we walk and work together in life. We empower and encourage one another. We pick each other up when one falls and call out to God for one another in all kinds of situations. We protect each other, often by just being there. As Philo Trust Associates, one of our early agreements was that we would never go alone when travelling and would be accountable to others at all times. These fundamental principles have kept me safe, and I am so grateful for all the people who have travelled with me over the years to some quite extraordinary situations.

At Ridley Hall Theological College we were encouraged, as we launched into ministry, to form an accountability support group that would meet as often as was possible. Peter Law, David Proud and I formed such a group. We meet every month for the inside of a day; we mainly chat and laugh and eat our way through some of the best pub lunches of England! We do pray, sometimes cry and have journeyed with each other for twenty-five years, hardly missing a month. Sometimes it has been tempting to allow something to get in the way of a meeting. Rarely has this happened, and when it has, we have all felt the disappointment of it. We know, trust, enjoy, pray for and increasingly deeply love one another. We have seen each other through triumphs and trials of the Christian life and leadership. On recent retirement, Peter has even moved near to David's new parish in Bedhampton so he can assist him when needed. This means that two out of every three months I get to visit coastal pubs for lunch with them in a new area! It's been amazing. We are not designed to go it alone.

We live in a church culture now where, sadly, there is little loyalty or support. People are often concentrating on their own needs, rather than looking to the needs of others. This is often seen in 'church drifting', where people constantly move on to other churches in order to provide for their own personal needs rather than the needs of others. They go to where the worship is better, or the preaching more biblical, or the people are more welcoming. They keep searching for the perfect church or the perfect pastor that will be best for them. It smacks of a wrong theology of church and sadly the American church is not helping us in this respect, where Christians church-hop constantly.

Often on teams away people learn to look out for each other and, in doing so, realise that others will naturally want to look out for them. Team members learn to prefer one another and not to just look out for themselves. This is another essential discipleship foundation.

Once I was away with a team, and a member had a terrifying psychological reaction to taking the drug 'Lariam' that they were using to ward off malaria. Few people use it these days because of this occasional side-effect. The reaction caused the person to change in personality, become incredibly volatile, wander off into the bush and become quite hostile towards the rest of us. From a team leadership point of view it was to this day the biggest challenge I have ever faced. The team member was in real danger and was putting the whole team at risk without desire or realisation. In the preparation that teams undergo, everyone is taught never to go alone, especially out into the bush. This team member, sadly, hardly knew what they were doing because of the effect of this very strong anti-malarial which most nurses and doctors in England are hesitant now to prescribe.

However, it was fantastic to see how the whole team coped with the challenge. They, in turn, missed amazing experiences and opportunities in order to give the person round-the-clock personal care. They loved deeply and prayed fervently for this team member in trouble. The situation had a huge impact on what we could do and the programme we were running. We were, in time, able to persuade the member to come off the Lariam, but they were basically ill for the rest of the visit and for some time afterwards. This was an extreme situation which I hope that not many teams or team leaders will have to cope with. But truly this team had "the back" of this person, and they could not fail to know this, even in the depth of the trauma they experienced.

This person got good medical treatment on their return to England, and it is wonderful to know that some years later this particular team member went on to work for Wycliffe Bible Translators. The experience certainly had not put them off at all.

I have used this simple phrase and tried to model it myself in my life ever since learning this from Gail many years ago. It has become a kind of catchphrase in church life, and I am so grateful for this because it has caused such fruitfulness in relational mission.

The fact is, bad things do happen to good and godly people. When they do, what will our response be? Will we be like Job's friends who gave inane, spiritual lectures of no use whatsoever – or will we do what Job really needed and sit with him on the ash heap and cry with him? Our churches and communities are full of broken people who need someone to let them know that you "have got their back." As this practical love is realised, experienced and begins to spread within a community, then spiritually anything can happen!

Action

1. Whose back have you got?

2. Who has got your back?

3. What benefit does this bring to your life?

4. How can we increase personal care and loyalty in our local churches?

5

Healing Happens

Healing/Loyalty

J John asked me to join one of his short-term mission visits to South India, and I was incredibly excited and privileged to go. As I reflect on this particular visit, I realise that I learned huge amounts from the way John led his team and the way the programme was so wisely managed.

We spoke and ministered in lots of different situations; we were looked after by our hosts wonderfully and given some amazing opportunities.

I cannot resist re-telling one funny story from this mission that has gone down in history among us as Philo Trust Associates. One evening we were having a very lovely dinner with a bishop in his house, and the electricity failed. Candles were lit and the meal continued. Food was being brought to the table, and at one point J John said to us quietly, "What are we eating?" (He has a severe nut-allergy and has to be very careful what he eats.) We discerned that it was a pure sesame seed ball, held together with honey! Realising this, two of us took J John round the back of the house with the excuse of going to the toilet and made him vomit what he had eaten so that he did not have an anaphylactic fit. That would have been OK, but it was pitch black outside and just where we chose for him to get rid of his food lay a sleeping dog in the undergrowth! The dog leapt at us, barked wildly, scared us half to death, and we ran back inside like crazy! We have laughed about this so often I can't tell you! Humour and fun on these mission visits bonds teams and reminds us that our faith journey does not have to be so serious all the time! Fortunately we did not have to pray for John to be healed on that occasion!

As part of this trip to India we were invited to visit and speak at the Roman Catholic Divine Retreat Centre at Chalakudy. This is a famous place of pilgrimage for thousands of Indians, as many of them find that God heals them there.

I could not believe my eyes – as far as I could see were human beings with relayed screens of what was happening from the front area. I have never been to such a massive Mass that was done so quickly but so beautifully! I had never spoken to so many people before, nor have I since!

As speakers came and went from the platform, the sick were then called forward to show the leaders how God had healed them. There was no 'ministry time', laying on of hands or a special team that did the healing. Either you were healed as the speakers or service occurred or you were not.

What the leaders required was for the healed to come to the front and for their healing to be verified by some waiting medical examiners. I watched mesmerised as callipers were taken off legs and people began to leap around. It was inspiring, as people who had been born blind could now suddenly see.

My belief in healing was cemented! I admit that before this experience I had believed in healing when I first became a Christian but, as so often with us in the medically knowledgeable West, I had begun to stop expecting healing when I prayed for it.

I have reflected on this a great deal over the years. When I first became a Christian in 1978, there were at that time some wonderful tent missions being led by an evangelist called Don Double. (That's given my age away!) There was one particular mission that he led in Shrewsbury that I had joined his team for, and I learned a great deal from him. One night Don believed that God was going to heal a woman with blindness in one eye and asked if there was such a woman in the gathering. We waited awkwardly – me thinking it was all a bit unlikely and, anyway, rather embarrassing! He persisted, and then up popped this lady who walked forward and onto the platform to be prayed with. He established that she was totally blind in one eye and could only see partially with the other eye. He asked her sensitively if he could cover her good eye up and then pray for God's healing to come to her. She agreed. I held my breath and felt cold shivers at what we were going to do pastorally when all this went wrong.

Don asked her if she could try to read with her blind eye – but she could not. So he prayed again, explaining that sometimes it took a few prayers. He asked her again to try to read and – to my absolute shock and amazement – she started to see. By the end of her time on that platform her sight was fully restored. God had healed this lady wonderfully, and she went into the local area and brought many to hear the good news of Jesus – many of whom came to faith that week. I discovered, as I got to know my Bible, that healing should be expected; it was very much part and parcel of the ministry of Jesus.

You might think that with biblical understanding and then the experience of this healing I might have become confident in this area. But the years had gone on and, in my experience of the local church, healing was not really on the agenda and was regarded as somewhat extreme. Gradually my expectation and therefore my practice at praying for healing slowly diminished. Is this your experience?

Suddenly I was in India seeing an explosion of healing. There was no doubt it was happening, and it deeply increased my belief that God heals today.

I learned so much from being at that Roman Catholic centre. On one occasion we were just walking as a team through the communal areas when a woman, who was literally lying on the ground beside us, shrieked and began to writhe around. We stopped, and the Indian priests took care of her as she settled. It was then explained to us that she had just been set free from demon possession, purely because she expected to be set free if she could get close to us. This excited but terrified me! How could I explain this at home? I would be misunderstood and be classified with the extreme, spiritual loony club! But isn't it great that on that day she was freed from evil? I wish over the years I had told this story a lot more. She expected to be released from that evil, and God honoured her expectation.

Some of the key lessons for me on that team were about the expectations of the people who wanted healing and the expectations of the retreat centre's spiritual leaders. The expectation that God could do it was tangible. Don Double's expectation was tangible. Does it always work? No. In Chalakudy, where there were hundreds of thousands of people, only some were healed. Jesus attracted huge crowds, but he did not heal everyone. Is it worth it then? Yes, because for those who were healed it has changed their life. And just as importantly, God has commanded us to...

Matthew 10:8

Heal the sick, raise the dead, cleanse those who have leprosy and cast out demons.

In the West, for all kinds of reasons, we have lost faith in the work of healing, let alone raising the dead or casting out demons. This desperately needs to change, and once again I would say that short-term mission experiences, where Christians can see the work of healing taking place, can restore faith and restore the practice of healing in the local church.

In going away on a short-term mission visit to India I returned with a confirmed, enthusiastic, expectant belief in God as healer – that it was not so much about the process of healing as it was that God could do it in any way He wants to. During the highest Mass I have ever attended at that centre, as the Host was lifted up, several people in the massive crowd were immediately healed! How can we explain that? If we do, we decide a process of healing which we then just repeat, hoping for the same again. Perhaps God will do that, but the point is that if the expectation is there on behalf of the person seeking healing, then the healing could happen. We seem to lay the responsibility too much on the pastor or process or place or principle.

Sometimes we need to go away to learn things that we can then bring home and enrich the local church with. This is certainly true in terms of the wonderful ministry of healing.

Action

1.   Read Matthew 20 verses 29-34.

2.   What is your view and expectation of healing?

3.   How do you express this in your life and in your local church?

4.   In what ways does our culture work against people believing in healing?

6

Prayer Works

Prayer/Calling/Modelling/Gifts

The invitation to lead a mission at St Andrew's University was an exciting one, and I was really encouraged to be involved with the Christian Union who had put so much effort, preparation and prayer into the run-up.

The meetings in the chapel, the student halls and cafés went well, and everyone was hugely encouraged by what God was doing as people responded to Jesus.

Quite near to the beginning of the mission I was invited to a prayer meeting being hosted by Malcolm MacDonald, one of the student missioners. As I entered the room the fervent prayer and the presence of God was powerful. No fumbling, preachy prayers but passionate, faith-filled calling out to a God they trusted would hear them There was an expectation and joy in prayer that I have rarely come across.

With prayer going on like that no wonder God was on the move at St Andrew's! When God's people pray, anything can happen! Through this prayer meeting I deliberately got to know Malcolm because he struck me as a man of deep faith and had the air of revival about him. I was impressed with the way he and his friend went out on the streets weekly, reaching out to people with the message of Jesus. I learned that Malcolm himself came from a wonderful Christian family, had been brought up in the farthest, northern parts of Scotland, where on his island he would practise preaching at an early age to the cows in the fields! I liked this man!

As the mission came towards a close I asked Malcolm to consider shadowing me for a year in ministry, if he ever thought that was something he would like to do. A few months later he rang and asked to meet me in London to further the idea. The end result was that Malcolm joined me at St Stephen's, Twickenham, as an associate on the staff there; he worked with me for a year in the work of evangelism and then stayed a further year to work more generally on the staff for the vicar, Andrew Watson. From there, Malcolm went forward for training for Anglican ministry, has served a wonderful curacy at St Barnabas in Kensington and is now the Vicar of St Mary's, Loughton, in North London! You will not be surprised to know that prayer and mission mark this man out. You never know who you will find when involved in short-term mission, and those involved in the mission team may well find spiritual gifts and callings that they never realised they had.

On one of my many visits to Donetsk in Ukraine I remember Deborah Millar joining me on one of my teams. She is a highly gifted and motivated believer in Jesus. Deborah was born with hands and feet that were not developed fully, and she has conquered these frustrations with amazing enthusiasm for life and ministry.

Whilst Deborah was in Ukraine she caught a passion for the East and ended up ministering in St Petersburg for several years, helping street children find homes and developing proper child-safety procedures wherever she worked. The courage she expressed and the total love for the children was amazing. My point is that her calling came from a short-term mission visit to Ukraine, and it has hugely affected her life. Now back in England she is a member of a Fresh Expression Church at Hampton Wick near Kingston and, when I visited there recently, guess what? Deborah was fully involved with the children, booking them into Kids' Church and it was obvious all the kids knew and already loved her. What happens when we go away deeply affects us when we return to the local church. This seems to be a lesson we really need to learn as church leaders and churches.

Malcolm and Deborah both represent many people I could talk about who by going on a short-term mission have discovered calling, gifts and dedication to God's local church.

Action

1. Complete the next two sentences and then discuss them with a friend:

    1) Prayer is vital because...

    ----

    2) Prayer would become more passionate in me if...

    ----

2. Discuss with a friend any experience you have had of short-term mission.

3. Write down the top three lessons you learned through being away.

    1)

    2)

    3)

4. What three reasons would you use to encourage others to go?

    1)

    2)

    3)

7

Everyone In: Every Member Ministry

Delegation/Participation/Value/Unity

We were invited by Bishop Enoch Drati of Arua in Uganda to bring a SOMA team for a diocesan gathering and some area outreach. The team was made up of lawyers, financiers, teachers, media workers and clergy. It was one of my first attempts at leading SOMA teams, and I was definitely learning as I went along. One of my challenges was the fact that my boss, the Rev Martin Peppiatt, was on the team!

As I prepared the team in the months before going I delegated everyone a job. Fortunately for me this comes naturally and, in fact, I enjoy seeing everyone feel involved. There is always plenty to do on any team; roles include spiritual tasks and practical jobs. Every member of every team is asked to prepare their journey of faith, in order to be able to share it, and a short Bible-based talk which would last fifteen to twenty minutes. For the clergy neither of these things was a problem; for others, sleepless nights were had! I always appoint someone to watch over the finances, another to look after health issues, another to do general pastoring, another to assist with travel arrangements, another to keep contact with home base with information or prayer needs, and another to organise that everyone on the team leads the daily 'team devotional time with God'. There are, of course, many other jobs as you journey, and it's vital as a leader to spot gifting, use it and involve people as fully as possible. I think this is the number one skill of any team leader.

In Arua this was seen clearly as the programme unfolded. Some were up front speaking whilst others were buddying the speaker; some were praying in the background and others were back at base looking after the victim of the goat curry from the night before! Everyone had a part to play, and there was a great deal of joy on that particular team.

One of the things that made us laugh out loud was towards the end of the cathedral meetings when the Bishop decided to give Martin and me some special presents: two live chickens! I had been brought up in the country and knew to hold its legs firmly and tuck it under one arm; Martin did not – and his chicken leapt around the cathedral with many people chasing! It was one of the funniest moments and we have laughed about it a lot ever since!

On another team in Tanzania we were trying to prepare a song together just after our devotional time. The idea was that we were going to sing it as part of the farewell. Something started to make us laugh, and every time we attempted to start singing again we folded with lung-killing laughter! It was fantastic fun. That laughter even carried on the next day. There is much fun to be experienced on such teams – and couldn't we do with a lot more of that in our local churches?

The teams that went to Donetsk in Ukraine were often big teams of between fifteen and thirty, and then it is even more important that everyone has a role. This invitation was to help physically build a church for one thousand people. There was no shortage of jobs, but some people are not suited to hard labour and so it was essential that they had jobs which still remained valued. One of my life friends, Gillian Harrap, has often come with me on teams to Donetsk, and the Ukrainians absolutely love her. On the odd occasion she did not come they would be asking where she was! Gillian is not best suited for building walls or mixing concrete – but she is amazing at looking after the workers, making sure people had drinks and, of course, she did what she was able to with the physical work. Gillian is a great example of a Christian with a loving, servant heart. At our home church she is one of the many who serve in the background but are rarely noticed and, sadly, sometimes not thanked enough for what they do. Gillians are what every church desperately needs.

I remember watching some of the team doing a fantastic job of some outside rendering on a wall. The job started by knocking off the rendering that had been put on wrongly and then re-rendering it properly. I really fancied having a go at this and managed to muscle my way in. What a disaster! Firstly I knocked off rendering that was not supposed to come off, and then my new rendering was not that good – so my team members had to correct my mistakes! It's best to leave jobs to people who know what they are doing and use your own skills where appropriate!

Whatever size the team is, there is the absolute need for everyone to be a full part of the whole visit. Each team member needs to be able to use the gifts they have got and use the gifts they discover en route!

This is one of the great joys and real fruits of such short-term mission ventures. It makes sure that all its participants are used to their full capacity, and in doing so people's capacity is often increased. This means that on return to their local church they often want to be more involved, and many ministers at this point will want to shout, "Hallelujah!"

If every church was built on the principle of 'every member ministry' then our local churches would look very different. Sadly it is often too few people doing too many jobs, becoming exhausted and withdrawing, having become cynical.

1 Corinthians 12:12

The body is a unit, though it is made up of many parts, and though all its parts are many they form one body.

This, I believe, is a key biblical concept and one which, if we can make sure each of us learns as a fundamental part of discipleship, would mean the church has more than enough workforce for all the activities of the Kingdom that God longs for. This famous chapter of 1 Corinthians spells out different gifts but at the same time emphasises the unity of the body of Christ, the Church. David Watson really taught and lived this, which is where I have picked it up from, apart from the scriptures. He really knew what it was to involve people fully at grass roots level, and I still refer constantly to his book 'I Believe in the Church.'

Action

1. Read 1 Corinthians 12 and write down what strikes you as important from this passage.

2. Make a list of ways in which you are involved in your local church.

   1)

   2)

   3)

3. Write down what your main areas of gifting are and then ask yourself if these are being used in your church.

   1)

   2)

   3)

8

Every Drop Counts

Ownership/Guidance/Parenting
Maturity/Giving/Mission

The enormous problem of HIV/AIDS throughout our world often causes people to feel defeated and think that little can be done. When people attempt to do something it has been said critically that it's "just a drop in the ocean".

My response to this has always been the same. Every drop makes up an ocean; it's vital we do something rather than nothing because what we do will help. It is to me the basis of our democratic system; if people stop voting because they feel their one vote counts for nothing, we are certainly in a mess.

I first came across the work of Gary and Marilyn Skinner when I invited their children's choir from Kampala to come and sing at St Stephen's Twickenham. This amazing couple has set up what is now known as *Watoto*. The fundamental mission is to rescue HIV orphans and give them homes, an education and health-care until they go to work or have completed university. They have approximately two thousand children in their care and have built several complete villages in Uganda that have homes, schools, healthcare and micro industries so that they can become self sufficient. I could tell you many stories about this wonderful work.

International teams go to one of the Watoto villages outside Kampala or in Gulu. The team finances, and then builds, either homes or classrooms. As a local church we have built three homes, and this year we are going to build our first classroom. Over a hundred and fifty different people have gone on these practical mission visits from our Anglican church of St Saviour's, Sunbury.

So many of our people have come back transformed by such visits, and this year sees our biggest team ever of twenty-five people going to Gulu. The team members get their hands dirty in the soil of Africa and work alongside the Ugandan builders to create homes for desperately needy children. They play football with the children, learn about their horrific stories and learn huge amounts of life in Africa. They eat the local food, learn a little Swahili and share their faith in all kinds of different ways during the visit.

We have encouraged parents to travel with a teenager on our teams. It has created a shared experience that has deeply blessed what can sometimes be a tricky relationship. My daughter went with her Mum and she said it was one of the most significant things she has ever done. Nicol's view of the world significantly changed, and she has a real heart to make a difference in her life, partly because of this visit. Parenting teenagers can be a very complex and difficult challenge. Choosing battles has to be learnt by the parent, but one of the greatest wins is having some shared experience or common interests. This summer my youngest teenager, Arran, will be joining my wife and I in Gulu. He has raised all of his own money to come which, in itself, is a huge encouragement to him, let alone what he will give and experience when he is there. Ownership partly comes through the team members raising their finances; ownership is crucial if the person is going to be able to fully give and receive from such an experience. We, as a family, will always have that time in Africa as something we can share together, so if times get tough at least there are some joyful times to reflect on. So once again you can see that by going away things are deeply affected at home.

One of our teenagers, Stephanie Andrews, was so struck with the visit with her Dad to a Watoto village, that she joined the new Discipleship Training Course that Watoto is now offering, based in Kampala. Steph was there for six months, and during this time she had a multitude of opportunities and experiences of mission alongside Ugandan Christians. I remember one of her emails telling us about how she had met terrible poverty in the slums of Kampala and how God enabled her to cope, serve and love in such situations. Steph has never been the same since. She preached in our local church on her return with such passion, maturity and confidence; she has found a direction in life that is heading her towards university to study to become a much-needed social worker in England. Steph is helping me lead this year's team, and her specific role is to enable a group of our women to minister to a new work of Watoto amongst women who have been horrifically abused by Joseph Coney's 'Lord's Resistance Army'. The work is called 'Living Hope', in which women's dignity and self-worth is restored by receiving plastic surgery, trauma rehabilitation, counselling and being trained in micro industries, so that they can earn income to raise the kids they have often received through rape. This work is so important. Medical help has been freely offered from all around the world, including England, to restore women who have had their noses, breasts or ears sliced off by machete by the LRA soldiers.

One abiding memory of Gulu is a wonderful room full of forty pedal-driven Singer sewing machines all working at full speed as women learn to makes clothes, bags and bangles to become self-sufficient. Every drop counts – perhaps you can get involved in this or another project somewhere in the world where you can make a difference.

We have had (and will have again this summer) whole families go together on a team. I have been advised against this because of team dynamics, but personally I think it's fantastic and it all depends on how the team is managed as to whether it works or not. The sacrifice of an annual, international package holiday by going on such a practical mission venture will never be regretted.

When the Watoto children's choir is on tour in England they usually visit our church, and these occasions are amazing. The children, with their adult supervisors, stay in church members' homes and sometimes even with their sponsors – which, when it happens, is terrific for sponsors to meet their kids and vice versa! The concerts are some of our most evangelistic moments of the year as the orphan children tell their story of despair and now hope; many local people are spiritually moved. People in these concerts come to faith, sponsor children and are drawn to churches which take direct practical action.

I had the privilege of being on the United Kingdom Board for Watoto for three years. During that time I saw the expanding work of this movement. The vision has grown so much that now Watoto villages and churches are starting in other nations such as Cape Town in South Africa. Gary and Marilyn Skinner have incredible vision and are able, because of the favour of God on their lives, to bring a lot of that vision to a reality and, in so doing, are making many children's and women's lives fruitful and full of God's purpose.

Many English mission organisations are finding things financially tough and that the number of financial donations is going down. This may be partly due to our economic climate but is perhaps more to do with a lack of connection with what the money is being used for. Short-term visits help the giver to understand, and have some relationship with, what they are giving to. I know that Tearfund has taken this on board and has all kinds of teams going out all around the world. I think this is very wise because people tend not to give in the long term to something that is cold, distant and difficult to relate to. Watoto has certainly learnt this, and perhaps other missionary organisations need to re-examine this possibility.

Sadly there has been much criticism of short-term mission, especially with the argument that so much money is used just to get a team member there. However, the person raises that money themselves, and in doing so it challenges and changes them in the most profound ways, the result of which is often that they are more committed to mission generally than they ever were before. This includes how they get involved in mission and financially give to it after their return. It also has a profound effect on their financial giving to their local church, especially if their churches are involved in mission at home and abroad.

I know that MAF is receiving gifts from some of my team members and their churches because they have experienced firsthand how that mission enables all kinds of aid workers to get safely into some of the most dangerous parts of the world. If you have ever flown with them, you automatically want to support them. I have had many adventures with their pilots and planes. One that directly comes to mind was a flight from Tanzania back to Kampala, when the pilot announced to us that he was unable to land because there was a storm sitting over the city and we would have to divert elsewhere. The team was not that happy; they were tired and wanting a rest night in Kampala before then getting back to England. The pilot said that there was no choice, barring a miracle. So that's what we went for – and as we prayed we literally watched the storm move so that we could see the airport and land with total safety! Prayer works!

Action

1. Discuss with a friend your reaction to the phrase "It's just a drop in the ocean."

2. What would stop you joining a short-term international team?

3. Discuss with a friend or partner what the value is of a parent going with a teenager on such an adventure.

4. Discuss with a friend what a difference it might make to your financial giving if you had more engagement with what a mission organisation or local church was directly involved with.

9

Polluted Lakes

Encounter/Character/Direction
Commitment/Dependence/Courage

On our many visits to Donetsk in the Ukraine we would always end up being invited to baptise, with the pastor, those who had come to faith in Jesus. This was always a great privilege and a huge personal blessing as people proclaim faith and then are baptised.

On several occasions I was warned not to enter the lake where these baptisms took place because they 'might' be polluted with radiation or chemicals by the many factories on the side of its banks. The water certainly had a murky look to it! But the over-cautiousness and critical nature of westerners I find difficult.

I remember being in India with J John and team and being asked to baptise a whole group of people in a swimming pool that was housed in a Leprosy Mission. The pool was pretty rank and the huge spiders with their webs that hung low over the pool certainly made my skin crawl. But we were asked to baptise people who had just come into relationship with Jesus – what a joy!

So we went into the Indian and Ukrainian waters and baptised God's people without ever falling ill. It was a great highlight of these visits and, as often happens, others came to Christ because of the shared testimony of those being baptised.

One of the things I have noted over the years on mission is that as people come to faith and are baptised it fires up all the Christians that see it happening. It renews faith. It increases expectation. It causes deep rejoicing and an increasing desire to see more people believe and trust in Jesus.

Stuart Murray, in his book 'Post Christendom', says the following:[2]

The future of the church in Western culture – and possibly even Western culture itself – depends on a fresh encounter with Jesus. An encounter with his example and teaching that inspires creative and counter cultural living ... unmasks the powers and gives hope for a different world... and energises hopeful discipleship.

So many times I have found team members encountering Jesus in a fresh way because they have stepped out of their comfortable lives and encountered Him in action around His world. This deeply affects character formation and is of great necessity if we are going to see deeply disciplined disciples of Jesus Christ.

Bishop Graham Cray, in an exciting new book called 'New Monasticism and Fresh Expression of Church'[3], makes a fascinating observation about character formation:

...character grows through making and sustaining wise choices ... the evasion of commitment is a recipe for permanent immaturity.

---

[2] Stuart Murray 'Post Christendom,' Authentic Media 2011
[3] Graham Cray 'New Monasticism and Fresh Expression,' Canterbury Press 2010

One of the real fruits of these visits is that members return with a clearer sense of direction, the ability and desire to make better life choices and a firmer commitment to Jesus and His local church. In a time where younger generations find commitment very difficult, we certainly need to take notice of the fruits of missionary ventures if it really does counter this unnerving culture of permanent immaturity.

When we are in a situation where we have no choice but to trust in God, we often have a fresh encounter with Him! We were in the middle of a very exciting meeting taking place with the Karamajong people of Uganda. The church was heaving with people, the Holy Spirit was moving in great power, and there was a deep sense of God's presence. Suddenly the church doors were literally thrown open. In walked this tribal chief with a machine gun over his shoulder. He strode to the front with great confidence, and as he arrived at the front of the meeting there was deep fear gripping everyone present. He just looked at us for a moment, puzzling what was happening. He then spoke, and my interpreter explained what he said:

Whatever you are doing here in the place you must continue. During the night my tribe and another local tribe, who have been at war killing each other for cattle for many years, have been reconciled to one another and we are now at peace. We have found that the atmosphere had changed and that it was something to do with whatever you are doing here. We need to know what this is about. Continue.

With that he marched out and some local Christian leaders followed him to explain what Christianity was all about!

That experience will never be forgotten by that team! One moment they thought life was going to come to a sticky end, and the next moment a heavenly party erupted on earth. It was an experience I personally have remembered often and was for me and others the cause of a fresh encounter with Jesus. We knew what it was to totally depend on God and His mercy in what seemed a most dangerous moment.

Action

1. Journal for yourself what your most recent encounter with Jesus has been.

2. Discuss with a friend what system of discipleship has helped you the most so far.

3. Discuss with a friend what discipleship system is presently used in your church.

4. Make a list of three things that you know will encourage deeper Christian commitment in young people today.

   1)

   2)

   3)

10

Too Much Choice

Consumerism/Materialism/Culture

One day after returning from Ukraine, my wife asked me to go and get some washing fluid, as we had run out, and some other basics. Simple task you may think! Obediently I set off for Tesco's at Twickenham by the rugby grounds. It felt strange driving again, and as I drove I was a little overwhelmed by being back in England. I parked the car, got my trolley and set off into the cathedral of a supermarket.

It really struck me how huge the shop was, how many aisles there were, and how many people were shopping frenetically! All went OK until I hit the aisle where all the washing fluids were – a whole row on both sides with the most enormous choice range of them. Why so many? I totally froze in the middle of that aisle – a customer even asked me if I was alright! It was for me a profound and disturbing moment, on which I have reflected often.

In Ukraine, just a few days before, I was in shops where the shelves in the stores were pretty empty and the choices of things were severely limited. As for washing fluid, there was of one kind only and it was very expensive because it was so rare. Here I was in affluent Twickenham with so many varieties of washing fluids it was absolutely absurd, and it caused a real mix of emotions. I got out of Tesco's as quickly as I could, headed for home and did some more debriefing work with Kim before I ventured out again!

This experience has taught me a great deal about how bad things have got in our consumerist culture and how we now have so many choices in front of us every single day of our lives. It certainly does not help us to remain committed to anything when we can just tour around all kinds of products or activities without remaining faithful to any. It ended up making me think long and hard about the way consumerism has affected how we view everything and what we are putting our trust in.

We were once travelling on a very uneven Ugandan track in the back of a truly beaten up, old Land Rover! My team, who were a real mixture of people from different walks of life, was literally being thrown around! One of the team was David Rowe, a very successful London businessman, who had adapted brilliantly into African culture; I had never seen him without a suit on in my life! As we tried to hold our dinner in as this Land Rover careered along, David turned to me and said, "I will never look at money in the same way." It seemed to come quite out of the blue, but in retrospect he had been reflecting on the terrible poverty that we had been ministering amongst and was hardly aware of how rough the journey was. David's life had been deeply challenged by being personally involved with real, in-your-face poverty.

For many years I have remembered David saying this, and it has struck me time and time again that we in the West desperately need to be more personally aware of what extreme poverty looks like and that a child dies of AIDS every three seconds. We hear the statistic – but does it really sink in? We hear so many statistics all the time and we become numb to them. But to go, visit and get involved in this essential work amongst poverty and such children is life-changing. We come back with a different perspective on our money, as David said, and we begin to use it much more wisely.

I am a real coffee drinker and have sadly become a little snobbish about quality. Not long after returning from Sudan a few months ago I was in one of our many English coffee houses and had another challenging personal moment. The lady at the till was asking me for £7.40 for a vanilla latte and a cake! She must have thought I had lost it when it took me a few moments to get over the shock of the cost and get my money out. Just hours before in Sudan I had been in a situation where some Sudanese women were boiling rice and cooking chicken (with the least meat on the bones I have ever seen); then they were putting portions into plastic bags and creating huge mounds of meals. They were feeding the local starving and providing food for prisoners who would have died without it. The cost was something in the region of £4 and they were literally rescuing hundreds of people. This really calls into question my coffee costs!

My mother has been holding coffee mornings for years for the work amongst women in Rwanda, especially since the genocide. Mum has raised many hundreds of pounds, and this is in itself a fantastic contribution. One day she received a phone call from the charity she had been raising money for, inviting her to join a team to go and visit some of the projects. Mum was stunned and excited. She said to me, "They can't realise how old I am; I may not even be able to get insurance!" Mum investigated the details, got her own insurance and went with them. Some of the visit was terribly upsetting as she learned from the locals the real story of all that had happened – it was chilling. But to have been there and met the people has made a profound difference in Mum's life. Mum has always been positive to an extent, but I have noticed an increase in that positivity since the visit. Going to these places makes a difference and, even if the team is just visiting, it means a huge amount to those receiving you, who need to know that others stand alongside them despite the air miles.

Bishop Graham Cray teaches brilliantly on consumerism when he talks about it being not so much what we buy but, more dangerously, the lens on life through which we see everything. We are in real trouble here in England, and many of us do not realise how deeply we have been affected. You will not be surprised then by my suggestion that going away, as I have often done, is wonderfully releasing and has enabled me to see life often very differently.

Water out of a tap remains now a miracle and a joy! Having such an amazing National Health System is a constant source of comfort to me. Having been in so many places where such basic things do not exist, I no longer take them for granted and work hard to enable those who do not have water or healthcare to receive them; hence my work with aid organisations such as Watoto.

Action

1. Make a list of everyday things we take for granted.

2. Discuss with a friend how consumerism has affected us and our way of life.

3. Look at your last two bank statements and ask yourself the following question: How much do my bank statements reveal my involvement in the activity of God's Kingdom at home and abroad?

4. Discuss with a friend what you could do if you are not able to join a team.

11

Who Can Go?

Risk/Vision/Testimony/Service

A team was forming to go with me to Cape Town in South Africa. It's not an unattractive place to visit so it was not that difficult to put a team together – a little different to creating a team for the Congo.

A couple of friends of mine, Carlos and Claire Clarke, were showing interest, and I was very keen to take them. At that particular time they had separated, after a short early spell of marriage had become terribly difficult for them. The opinions as to whether it was right to take them or not massively collided. Personally, I sensed God calling me to be committed to this couple for the long haul and that it would be brilliant all round if they came. Some Christians, as usual, doubted my motives as Carlos is a diamond at visual drama and Claire an incredibly anointed worship leader and speaker! It was not because of their gifting that I took them. No one is perfect; everyone has issues and it is so sad to judge people so badly that they then miss opportunities that would actually help them at deep discipleship levels.

They both came and they both saw the hand of God working in Cape Town. It was not the only thing that helped them repair their marriage, but it was certainly a part of it. People believing and trusting them despite their difficulties made a huge difference. Today they are a mature Christian couple with two fantastic, creative children who love Jesus. Their discipleship is unquestionable. Carlos is making a huge impact in his witness in the police, and Claire is my Worship Director and Assistant Pastor, whilst training at St Militus for ordained Anglican ministry. They have, until recently, been leading one of the most fruitful small groups in our church that I have ever witnessed. They care for and love people at a deep level. They live community like I rarely see and use their time in the most fruitful ways. I am not saying they are perfect because that would not be true, but as excellent examples of disciples you would be hard-pushed to find better - and especially in their 30's age bracket.

One of our experiences in Cape Town, that affected many of that team, was the discovery with the local people of the vision God had for them. We were prayer-walking through one particular, very difficult area and, as so often happens, God spoke supernaturally through the ordinary things of life. Just below the pavements we were walking on, a teeming river was flowing, and every now and again grates in the paths revealed the water flow. God spoke to all of us about a time coming when living water would burst out and bring a real, spiritual harvest to that area. The locals were really excited and some were called into ministry because of that release of vision. The experience also taught my team members about how vision comes and to be more open to how God speaks. Vision is essential for life and ministry. It is essential for the local church, and if short-term visits like this encourage vision, then let's do more of them!

We Christians are one family all over the world, and when one part of this amazing family invites another part to come and help them, why would we only send the perfect? And, in any case, by whose standards is anyone perfect? I have more often found that those who have struggles and are willing to share them openly and honestly relate to people everywhere more effectively than victorious proclaimers.

On one team my great life friend, Gillian Harrap, shared about her depression in a Ukrainian environment. Here in England that would not have been a problem as it's culturally understood and cared for. In the Ukrainian context it was unacceptable, especially amongst those we were ministering to. The tension was tangible! I spoke and backed up what she had said, and there followed a time of ministry that was so healing, as people for the first time began to open up as to how depressed people were.

If you were asked to make washing machines that you knew would not work – and for which there was no market – how would you feel?

That's what it is like in parts of Ukraine today; economically things are hard and many are depressed. I was actually shown the stockpiles of washing machines that were going nowhere.

If you were not allowed to have anyone visit your house without there being huge suspicion about you and your family from the Communist regime, how would you feel? For many years this is exactly what it was like in Ukraine. It created incredibly strong family units, which is a really strong part of Ukrainian culture now, but it had an oppressive effect on people's lives; depression is rife – yet no one is allowed to admit it.

Even worse is the dreadful, 'spiritual' attitude in some church denominations where depression is considered satanic. It is therefore dealt with as such by some Christians in that culture; if ever you admit that you have depression or something like it, you find yourself being 'delivered' rather than cared for with sensitivity.

I am glad to say that today things are changing, at least in the contexts of where we were ministering, and God's people now care for the huge number of depressed people in that city of Donetsk. This, in part, is due to one fragile, broken team member being willing to share her struggle with depression, which had gone on for many years, and the way that God has enabled her to live well.

Gillian is well known to the people of Donetsk, and they always hope that she is on the next team. In no way did things close down on her because of what she shared; in fact, quite the opposite! For Gillian, going away on these missionary ventures has been part of her discipleship journey, and through them she has been changed by God immensely. From the quiet mouse that she was at university to the confident Maths teacher who holds her own and ministers weekly in our local church, you can see the fruitfulness that is, in part, due to such visits.

Like many of my age, I have been hugely affected by David Watson's life and writings. As I write on this theme of how mission helps create mature disciples like Gillian, his work and words are often coming to mind. In his book 'Discipleship'[4] he gives us twenty-one marks of what

---

[4] Page 75

he regards as a disciple, and I think they are incredibly relevant today. Here they are in a summarised form put as questions:

1. Are they willing to serve?
2. Are they learning to listen?
3. Are they willing to learn?
4. Are they willing to be corrected?
5. How well do they submit to authority?
6. Can they share their life with others in open, honest fellowship?
7. Are they learning humility?
8. Are they self-examining before criticising others?
9. Are they a perfectionist?
10. Are they aware of their weaknesses?
11. Are they able to forgive?
12. Do they have stickability to a task?
13. Can they be trusted?
14. Do they mind their own affairs?
15. Do they do small things well?
16. How do they use their leisure time?
17. Are they living to firstly please God?
18. Do they swiftly respond to the call of God?
19. Is there evidence of faith in God even when things are tough?
20. Where is their security?
21. Do they possess a clear understanding of God's priorities for their life?

These questions are an amazing MOT for all of us, whether we have been Christians a short while or, like me, for thirty-three years. As I read these checkpoints, I realise once again where my discipleship is weak and where it is stronger.

Stop for a moment. Read all twenty-one questions again and grade yourself – 1 being low and 5 being high – as to how you are in response to each. Prioritise your top five areas for encouragement! List your lowest five areas so that you know what to be working at!

As I re-examine this helpful list, I am so excited to be able to share with you that most of these twenty-one areas can be greatly helped by most short-term missions. I have witnessed it firsthand, where members become willing to serve because of the needs they see in front of them and, in doing so, prove that they are willing to learn. I have witnessed the increase in people's ability to listen to one another and share with each other at a much deeper personal level. Teams learn to be responsive to authority, accept criticisms and become more humble in spirit. In the face of some tremendous expectations they realise their weaknesses, accept their own limits and learn to do what they have been asked to do well for the glory of God, rather than the seeking of personal praise. They often learn to be loyal and build one another up, therefore becoming more self-aware and less critical. They learn to stick it out, however bad the toilets in Africa are, or however steep the challenges. Team members learn to be quick to respond to what God is doing and calling them to do and, in doing so, God increases their faith. Teams come home with the realisation that every moment matters, and this hugely affects how they use their work and leisure time. Their trust in God for everyday things is heightened, and therefore their security is increasingly upon God rather than themselves or their culture. Daily priorities often become clearer as perspective floods back – by simply being away in a different context but more so by seeing the work of God around His amazing world, where His Spirit is always at work.

Action

1. Share with a friend your top five and your lowest five of your discipleship score; then talk about them together.

2. Discuss how you might move forward in the weak areas.

3. Write down a personal vision statement for your life.

4. Articulate to a friend what your church's vision is and listen to their church's vision.

12

Rescue Job

Expectations/Programming/Unity/Abandonment

A few years ago I was asked to rescue a team because they had lost their leader through ill health and there was a danger of the invitation never being taken up and some disappointment in those who had been planning to go. After consulting with my wife, I decided this was something that I could do and so planned a couple of team meetings.

My worship leader, Claire Clarke, joined the team, which was very helpful to me as I had at least one person I knew and that I had worked with before in many different situations. Several team members decided not to come because the original team leader was not going, which is quite understandable if they were people that were going partly because of relationship with them. That left three people, and Claire and I made the team up to 5 members.

Our first team meeting was interesting! It became clear to me that this was going to be a huge challenge for all kinds of reasons. The age difference was from eighty to thirty-sixyears; there were three strong church leaders, and previous expectations were loaded onto this new team. One of the team members needed everything to be sewn up tightly so that they could plan carefully before going. This is, of course, quite understandable – some people find security in very tight schedules – and yet I knew that most of my experience of Africa was that the plan would unfold as we journeyed spiritually with the local people that we would be working with. I set the plan so that they could prepare and at the same time asked everyone to remain as flexible as possible.

Communications came before and during the mission from the original mission leader – some were informational and helpful. His disappointment in not going was more and more obvious, and so he was perhaps trying to affect what was going to happen. This created all kinds of tensions and involved one of the team members quite deeply.

Some perhaps would argue that coming up against some of these things before I went should have persuaded me to give up on it and cancel the visit. However, it is not in my nature to give up and, anyway, I sensed that something good was going to come out of what was a very complex situation.

Our second team meeting was very tense at the start, but eased considerably as the afternoon progressed. Preparation of any short-term team is vital, and I generally try to have several times together before we fly. On this occasion we even had a telephone link, as one of our team lived in Scotland and was therefore unable to make the long, expensive journey for team preparation. We started to mould together as a team.

The original team leader was at Terminal 5 with a few of the other original team to meet us when we were gathering to fly. It felt a little awkward, but after praying for us the original leader then gave me papers, books and presents to deliver to people where we were heading. Then, after some further moments, he graciously let us go!

I am writing about this because as part of our discipleship we need to learn how to handle tensions and conflict. I have always seen that many creative things can come from conflict handled well. Grace is a desperately needed characteristic in the Christian and in the local church.

As we made our way to the plane, a couple of us on the team began to laugh at the whole challenge. Here we were, the most diverse of characters you would ever meet, with tensions and a mixture of expectations. I laughed with my colleague Claire until it hurt. God was going to have to do something of a miracle to bring this together, and I deeply sensed He would!

As so often is the case in Africa, when we arrived in Tanzania the plans and needs expressed were hugely different to most of the information received, and as a whole team we threw ourselves into the arms of God so that He would lead us. This was the start of an amazing miracle of unity and spiritual fruitfulness that I have never experienced before or since. We learned to lean on God alone and each day would discern the way forward together.

One day of the visit I will never forget was when the local bishop suddenly started to repent publicly of his anger in front of all his colleagues and staff and it triggered a time of general repentance and Holy Spirit ministry. Heaven kissed the earth that day. One of our team shared personally, sacrificially and deeply on one of the days, and once again there was an outpouring of the Holy Spirit afterwards with many people being released, healed and blessed by God. If we had kept to our tight schedules, neither of these two incredible moments would have happened. I wonder how often we organise God out of situations where we are longing for Him to break in.

The age difference did not matter, the worship styles did not matter and the history of the team leadership did not matter. God was pouring out His blessing on the situation, and we just wanted to serve Him as best we could. I have never known a mission time go so fast, and when it was completed I felt grieved to say farewell to this particular team. I met one of them recently at a conference and, because of the depth of experience together, it was as if we had only seen each other the day before – the depth of feeling for each other was so great.

If only this could be our experience in the local church, where there is so often such tension and difficulty. These have their roots in so many issues, not least previous leaders, wrong expectations or variance of worship style. We need the Spirit of God to come down and bring His unity to the body. One of the great lessons we learned in Tanzania was full submission to the plans and will of God. Abandoning previous expectations and man-made plans was a key.

Action

Discuss with a friend:

1.　How heavily do I depend on God on a daily basis?

2.　How far do I submit to the will of God for my life?

3.　How flexible am I as to God's direction day by day?

4.　Do I bring unity wherever I go?

5.　How accepting am I that God's church needs to be made up of different people from myself?

13

The Wing Nut's Loose!

Laughter/Fear/Surprise

The road journey from Kiev to Donetsk was something in the region of twenty to thirty hours on roads you would not believe! So on one of the later visits we decided to pay for an internal Ukrainian flight to Dnepropetrovsk, only four hours away from our destination.

The Austrian Airways flight to Kiev was, as usual, wonderfully comfortable and straightforward. Then we experienced a different sort of air travel! As we boarded an internal flight we could see immediately that standards were different. Some of us sat in seats that were literally collapsing, not all of us had belts that worked and when the engines started so did the uncontrollable, nerve-charged laughter of the team. We were really scared and that fear was expressed, and to an extent released, by laughing.

As we looked out on the plane's wings, we could literally see nuts holding the plane together shaking and loose. Then the air hostess made her way down the aisle – never have I seen anything so funny. Her uniform was dishevelled, she tottered along in high heeled but unstable shoes, and her trolley – which looked like something from the 1960's – was bent and buckled. To this day I cannot remember what she was dishing out; all I can remember was the pain in my lungs and chest from the immense amount of laughter that went on! It was the whole team laughing, and the crew just assumed we were mad English abroad who were excited about where we were going!

On every trip laughter has been a wonderful gift to the team. Once, in Tanzania, it was caused by trying to practise a song that we had been asked to perform. On another occasion it was the knowledge that leopards had visited in the night just next to where we were sleeping! On a further occasion it was the seemingly impossible make-up of the team we were travelling with!

Laughter releases people. It releases fear and anxieties. It releases joy deep in the soul. It brings team unity. It is a real gift of God, and we need it wherever we are in the world, not least in our local church situations. If only we could laugh together more.

I realise it's not something that can be organised, but it is something that we can set the scene for. We can create environments where a lot of fun and laughter can be made possible. I have rarely had a team where laughter has been scarce!

Recently in our church we decided to have a big church 'social' because we were aware of needing more time to relax together and have more fun. Loads of planning went into this event, which was themed as a Hoedown with Bucking Bronco and Line Dancing etc. What I never found out was that the whole church was in on a secret, without me as leader knowing. For about nine months they secretly organised the event as a surprise fiftieth birthday party for me and, in doing so, fulfilled the need also for a whole church social. I was hoodwinked. Every week I was – without knowing it – selling the idea to the church of coming to my own surprise birthday party. People laughed as I announced it, and I never caught on why there was such fun about the event. I just assumed that we were doing a good job of selling the idea and that it was going to be all we imagined it to be as a social occasion!

The day arrived and I was setting up the church as we had planned as a team. As far as I am concerned as a leader, I never ask anyone to do something that I am unwilling to do myself, and so I was with everyone else putting up bunting and getting the whole church building ready. I had told the team that I could only help until midday because at that point I was to go and babysit for some good friends up the road whose mother had a hospital visit. Off I went to look after the wonderful Sterry kids, making gingerbread men with them and decorating them ready to eat!

Kim, my wife, was supposed to be coming to help me, but she had got caught up at the Open Morning she had been involved with in her school – and so I waited. Eventually, having got the children off for their midday nap, Kim turned up; we had some lunch and a game of scrabble. I started to feel uneasy as the time was passing and I knew I needed to be back at the church before the doors opened for the church social. A text came through from the kids' mother saying she was held up in Bushey Park in traffic, that she was terribly sorry but would be there as soon as she could. I totally swallowed that, as she is a very reliable friend and Christian!

On the mum's arrival, Kim and I made our way down to the church, a short seven-minute walk. I noticed as we walked that some familiar people were walking in the same direction; I should have smelled a rat, but Kim asked if we could just detour off the route for a moment whilst she looked at something. I was itching to be with my team but trying to be patient!

Kim and I arrived at the church, went through the front doors and literally hundreds of church family members of all ages cheered me in and sang Happy Birthday! They had re-organised the whole church since I had left at midday and had totally hoodwinked me! The laughter and joy of line dancing, a bucking bronco machine, BBQ, face painting, crafts and generally partying was huge!

Somehow the secret had in itself caused a lot of fun, and the event created the opportunity and atmosphere of a great deal of joy. We need this as part of church family life.

My church staff team and I generally have a lot of fun. I am on sabbatical as I write this book, but they met for their weekly team meeting as usual in the cottage attached to my house. Through very thick stone walls I could hear them joking and laughing together. I think it's a sign of a really healthy team that can do this.

Many of my team members have experienced real joy and laughter on their times away. It reminds them of the importance of this aspect of life, and I am sure that on return to their families and local church they are a greater blessing because of it.

Action

Journal the following:

1. How important is laughter and joy in the Christian life?

2. What could be done in your life and local church to bring more joy?

14

More Boot Removers, Please!

Ownership/Finance/Team

Arran is sixteen, he is just completing his GCSEs and has a part-time job for two hours a week. How on earth is he going to raise the £1,700 needed to take him to Africa to build a classroom for HIV orphans?

With two months to go he has raised £1,300, and when the exams are over he will be able to take up orders that he has got from the Christmas Craft Fair at church to start raising the rest of his money! Arran has made wooden boot removers, door stops and candle holders. He has given 50% of his weekly earnings of £20 and he has been a Wedding Assistant at church and given those payments into his fund. He has written to all his relatives, explaining what he is doing and asking for some sponsorship from them. He has helped at a church car wash and has even had his girlfriend's mother making cards to sell for him!

Arran was 'owning' what he is wanting to participate in – rather than hoping some generous benefactor will just gift him the money. Ownership is vital if you are going to get the most out of the visit. It's so true generally in life and increases personal responsibility.

Kim and I have made sure all along that we will help and support him so that the challenge does not overwhelm him but at the same time have encouraged him to try to do it himself. Challenges like this can be an opportunity for growth in maturity and character; after all it certainly didn't do Richard Branson any harm! Arran is already rightly encouraged by how far he has got in raising his finance in order to go.

Steph, another teenager in our church, decided to make cakes! You might think this would take forever to raise the finance she needed but not at the rate she made cupcakes and not at the rate her dad sold them in the workplace! On one of Steph's visits to Africa nearly all her money was raised in this way!

Our church has had some really good socials, as short-term mission teams have held fundraisers such as jazz nights, quizzes, dinners, concerts and Christmas fairs. Every church needs social time together and so it's been great both ways – we have had fun and the teams have raised some finances for the visits. So this has been great for our church in terms of deepening our friendship levels and has also created a congregational ownership of the visit itself. This has been so positive; it has meant that for those who cannot, for whatever reason, go on a short-term visit they still feel personally involved. This is something that the larger mission agencies would do well to realise because ownership creates commitment, which in turn produces support – including finance.

Team members take responsibility for their personal costs, and the joint team efforts, like car washing, raise the money needed for the cost of building or other visit-related activities.

Some of our church, who are unable to go because of age or health, have been very generous to team members. This has been wonderful, especially for some of the teenagers going, and produces the opportunity of relationships in the church family that otherwise may never have started.

Some of the businessmen that have come along have found that their businesses will match-fund what they raise personally, and in this way they have been able to raise a lot of finance. This is well worth investigating and has since proved very fruitful for general church giving as well. Some firms are more than happy to match-fund what their employees give to what they see as charitable works – church treasurers take note!

Over the years we have found that people love to support such practical team visits to the two thirds world. Individuals and businesses often send money a little after the visit has taken place! But this helps start a pot for the next venture.

Action

Discuss with a friend:

1.   What three ways could you raise the money to go on such a visit?

2.   How might your church respond financially or by prayer to you joining such a team?

3.   What positive effect could fundraisers have on your church's life?

15

Holy Moments

Spiritual Pathways/Renewal/Encounter

A spontaneous time of worship happened late one evening in the desert region of Karamoja. It was so uplifting and we all realised afresh the presence of the Creator. The stars shone, galaxies could be seen and team members would suddenly excitedly spot another star, announcing it to everyone! It was one of those moments that will never be forgotten.

The announcement that there was a white scorpion really near to my feet that night as we worshipped was something else I remember clearly!

In the Western world, for a multitude of reasons, we lose our way and need help to find spiritual direction. The work of Gary Thomas in his book 'Sacred Pathways' is incredibly helpful in this respect and, as I have reflected on the above experience and on many other moments whilst travelling away, I realise that to come on these mission ventures is a golden opportunity to get close to God again.

Gary describes nine sacred pathways that could help you discover your soul's way back to God or even find Him for the first time:

- *The Naturalist* whose cathedral is, for example, the clear, starlit African night sky.
- *The Sensate* who is helped to realise God through sights, sounds and smells such as the African soil.
- *The Traditionalist* who needs more historic forms of faith such as rituals, symbols, sacraments and sacrifice, such as the liturgical services in many African cathedrals.

- *The Ascetics* who want nothing more than to be left alone in silence and prayer. They love to visit places such as Prayer Mountain in Uganda.
- *The Activists* who discover God through calling people to faith and facing confrontation. They are energised more by interaction with others than being alone and Build Teams abroad suit them well.
- *The Caregivers* who realise God's love by loving others deeply, such as working in the 'Bullrushes' baby care unit or with abandoned or orphaned babies in Kampala with Watoto.
- *The Enthusiasts* who need excitement and mystery in worship so as to encounter God. They come alive in the more Pentecostal worship of many parts of Africa!
- *The Contemplatives* who seek to love God with the purest, deepest and brightest love imaginable; they see God as their lover.
- *The Intellectuals* who can only realise God through their minds for their hearts to come alive spiritually. They need to be studying things like Calvinism or predestination! They love to teach in the theological colleges or refresh spiritual leaders through biblical teaching.

It's truly a miracle that 'Church' works in any part of the world because in every fellowship you always have a mixture of all these avenues by which people find God! No wonder we get certain types of denomination. One of the many great strengths of Anglicanism is that it offers all of these pathways under the umbrella of one denomination whereas others use only a few of them. One of the important tasks is for Christian leaders to teach these pathways so that their people stay close to God. I have found an alarming number of evangelical Christians losing their faith, or at least going very cold spiritually, in their forties to fifties.

I have witnessed firsthand team members coming alive to God through these different pathways experienced whilst away from home, and it's a privilege to see it – Enthusiasts coming alive in exciting, African Pentecostal services; Caregivers being overwhelmed by the love of God as they nurse the baby just rescued from a bin in Kampala; and Activists re-encountering God as they build the classroom for HIV orphans. In so many ways these visits offer the team member the opportunity to receive perhaps far more than, or certainly as much as, they will give.

Action

1. Journal which your preferred spiritual pathway is.

2. Discuss with a friend how you could build time into your coming week/month to enable this pathway to be explored more fully again.

16

What One Team Said

Summer of 2011 held a fantastic opportunity to do once again what I have been writing about in this book. I took twenty-eight people with me to Gulu in Uganda to build a classroom on a Watoto village that houses HIV orphans, and we also did some work with the abused women of that area. The team mainly came from our own church of St Saviour's, Sunbury, but some were from other churches and one member was from Canada! The visit was for fourteen days, which included all the travelling necessary and a thirty-six-hour safari in one of Uganda's incredible game reserves.

In this chapter I am recording from personal interviews what individual team members have said they gained from this type of short-term mission experience. There is some real spiritual gold in what team members have said here; it is very worthwhile reflecting on the comments of each one. Just recording them has been such a blessing to me personally.

Coleen Entner from Canada

Colleen wanted to go once again to Uganda, having been once before on a Build Team, because her first experience so profoundly affected her. Once again, because of this summer's visit, she felt that her spiritual life had been sharpened by African spirituality and sensed more personal, spiritual awakening.

Colleen worked this time with the abused women who had seriously been messed up by Joseph Coney's 'Lord's Resistance Army'. Working with girls who had had their noses, ears, breasts and sometimes lips severed by this cruel army was a real challenge to her. It pushed her in terms of capacity and took her way beyond her personal comfort zones. There was one particular lady with a young child that Colleen was able to make a real connection with, and in watching how important this was to them she realised herself how rewarding this type of experience is.

Colleen is now considering other visits to Sudan and Rwanda.

Louise Fisher

Louise has visited Watoto Uganda on four occasions and this time went as a section team leader for the work amongst abused women.

Louise is certain how important it is to make the personal connection with what you are giving to financially. She said that it provides firsthand knowledge of what you are contributing to, which in turn, even more importantly, enables you to develop a relationship with the people or situation.

Louise has realised that to build houses, classrooms or enable women to be restored emotionally, spiritually and physically is achievable – that we can, when we work together, raise the funds necessary and keep going to make a real difference in people's lives. We in the West are so rich in comparison to the majority of this world. Louise feels that God has given so much to her that by being personally involved in Africa she is able to give something back to Him. It has become part of her offering.

When she is away like this she really enjoys the focus it brings, losing all the normal distractions of life and depending on God so much more. This then challenges her to live a more directed life when back at home.

Louise feels that for many people it is achievable to offer fourteen days to such visits. If Americans can do this when their vacation allowance is so much less than in Europe then surely it is easier for us! Louise is sure that if everyone did their little bit towards these huge problems like HIV, we would be able to change much in our world. She has seen it with her own eyes.

One of Louise's reflections on building the classroom is that it will stand for years to come and create the environment for the education of hundreds of children.

Louise is a child sponsor, and because of her visits she has been able to see the child several times on her visits to Africa. This personal connection makes the activity of sponsorship so much more real and therefore long-lasting. One of the great problems of child sponsorship is that people start enthusiastically and then after two to three years they stop altogether. This creates big problems for charities like Watoto. It is Louise's view that with a more personal connection would encourage a much longer-lasting commitment.

Gillian Harrap

Gillian is a long-standing Maths teacher in The Green School in Isleworth. She trained with me as a teacher in the 1970's Gillian has travelled with me many times, mainly to Ukraine, but this summer was her first visit to Africa.

Gillian went as part of the 'Living Hope' team to work amongst abused women, and she felt that to form a relationship with the situation and people rather than sending money coldly was really important in terms of long-term interest. She also felt it was important for her to be taken out of her comfort zones so that God could stretch and change her.

Gillian's firsthand involvement in the traumas of these women has had a big effect on her perspective of life here in England. She realised that the women in Gulu appreciated what seemed like small things to her – for instance, physical touch or being taught to make simple headbands.

Gillian had researched on the internet what she was likely to face in terms of the physical sight of some of the victims she would be dealing with. This was typically wise of Gillian, and it meant that when she was there she could see the real women behind their terrible injuries. The importance of the restoration of these women's self-worth and identity cannot be overstated. This can be done by plastic surgery, psychological rehabilitation and by being taught work skills – all of which is happening because of the wonderful work of Watoto. But just as important is the acceptance and personal love of another human being. The women of Gulu are constantly amazed that Western women will save up their money and fly so far away to just spend time with them. It means a huge amount to them. She reminded me that one of the most powerful effects of

Princess Diana's life was that she would hug the child or adult who had HIV/AIDS. She also reminded me in this interview that Jesus himself would touch the leper and eat with the outcast of society.

She, like Colleen, found that African spirituality was personally wonderfully refreshing and enlivened her own faith. She found working with the team was a helpful way, as a single person, to get to know members of her own church much more deeply. She saw this as a real fruit of the visit.

Gillian believes that teams going encourage more teams to go in the future because of the stories, experiences and films that are brought back to the local church.

Colin Agar

Colin has been one of my main team administrators and has assisted with the financial side of most of our visits to Uganda. This summer it was his sixth Watoto visit! He first went on an international Watoto Build Team and ever since then has joined teams from our church.

He believes that by going to the actual place it demonstrates our willingness to partner with the Africans. He feels that it's about 'being alongside' more than distance giving. He thinks that firsthand experience and 'getting your hands dirty' is much more fruitful in the long term. He sees that walking alongside gives you a deeper sense of the nature and magnitude of the real problems of Africa, such as the problem of child soldiers.

Colin has come to the spiritual realisation that we also have so much in common in all kinds of ways that you can only realise by being there and by being involved – that we are truly brothers and sisters in Christ, the common ground from which amazing relationships can be founded.

Guy Trevithick

Guy took his whole family on team to Gulu this summer; this included his wife, Jane, and their two teenagers, James and Katie. This is something I have tried to encourage over the years because it brings adventure to parents with their teenagers – a shared experience that is incredibly positive in a time when things can be tense in family life! Guy is a businessman who works for the tea company Twinings and is in his 40's.

Guy sensed that the experience enlarged his vision of God. He offered a question in the interview: by going to Africa, is it a deposit or a withdrawal from your spiritual bank account? His response was that by going it is certainly a deposit; an example of this would be that he sensed a huge deposit of compassion put into him as a person.

Guy felt that the visit changed his perspective on life in all kinds of ways. He also realised that the building of a house or classroom was vital in itself but also a mechanism to come alongside the people of Uganda. He said that friendship is maintained by seeing your friend, not just by stating that someone is your friend.

Jane Trevithick (Guy's Wife)

Jane joined the team with some apprehension of how it would all work out and whether sharing life with so many would actually be possible! She was really surprised at the unity, interaction, fun, delegation and ease that there was amongst us all. She really enjoyed the team experience, having suspected that she might not! This is a common fear, but most often teams that focus outside of themselves experience tremendous unity within.

Jane felt that by connecting with real situations and real people's individual lives in Africa, the passion to be more involved increased. She felt that this passion affected her spiritual life on returning home. This, in turn, affects the spiritual fruitfulness of who you are, wherever you are. She also experienced more of what it is to be truly dependent on God for people and situations in terms of prayer. She saw such direct answers to prayer during the visit that it has been a great encouragement to her own prayer life.

Jane learned in Africa that it really does take a 'whole village to bring up a child' – an African saying – and she wonders how this could relate more to our situation at home.

James Trevithick (Guy and Jane's son)

James learned how to make bricks and drive a mini JCB! He and the other teenagers on the visit had a lot of fun and really connected with the Ugandan young people – especially playing football in the midday sun! James learned what it meant to be one family of God wherever in the world you are, that the Africans he met were truly his brothers and sisters in Christ.

James feels that now he cares much more deeply for the situations in Africa rather than the cold distant feelings he had when he has previously watched reports on the television.

Katie Trevithick (Guy and Jane's daughter)

Katie was the youngest member of our team and was incredibly brave to be on the 'Living Hope' team working amongst abused women.

This experience for Katie was transforming. She said that on the plane out to Africa, all she wanted to do was to watch films; on the way back she just wanted to make a difference in life and really "do something worthwhile."

Kirsty Robinson

Kirsty works in the fashion industry and while she was in Gulu used her skills to teach the women to make headbands – which the women really loved and immediately started making and selling so that they could feed their children.

This was Kirsty's first visit of this kind and it has had a very deep effect on how she now lives her life here in the West. She told me that it took her out of her comfort zone, opened her eyes to what real poverty was and brought new perspective into her own life. She realised that westerners just continually want more, but she was beginning to realise that the love of God and His provision is enough.

She could see how thirsty for God people in Uganda are, how much they trusted God for their everyday needs, and she noted how much more relatable a lot of the Bible is to African life, because of its imagery, than it is to London life.

Kirsty noticed God stretching her capacity to be able to work in such a challenging environment. The first day she felt terrible, wracked with nerves and awkward. She then realised that she was not there for herself but to serve others, and as she got stuck into the work she just loved being there.

Kirsty would now love to serve again on a team in the future.

John Robinson (Kirsty's husband)

John is a policeman and this was his first visit to Africa on such a team.

He felt that it was humbling to see the love for God Ugandans have when, in the face of all that they suffer, they could so easily be cynical and angry with Him. He was blown away by their love and compassion in the context of their own suffering.

John found being there amongst God-dependent believers a huge inspiration. He felt that the visit challenged him on English values and the Western, materialistic life.

He really enjoyed getting to know members of his church more deeply by being on a team and thought the unity of the team was something very special.

Kim McDougall (My wife!)

This was Kim's second Watoto team visit; the first time she took our daughter, and this time she was with me and our youngest son!

Kim sees that, by going, it opens your eyes to the fact that in Africa their main concern is to eat, drink water and have clothes to wear. Their lives depend on these basic needs, and many only have the clothes they wear and food for that day. It's a day by day existence. For Kim this challenges the materialistic culture in which we live.

Kim finds that Ugandan Christians are genuinely happy people, not sorry for themselves, whereas she finds English people who have so much are continuously sorry for themselves and live a 'hard done by' existence.

Kim reflects that the more you see, the more you want and then the more you have. Where there is less choice there is less stress. She sees that many Ugandan Christians are truly contented, much more than she finds amongst English Christians.

Hannah Bowen

Hannah is a teacher, and this was her first visit to Africa.

Hannah wanted to give feedback that going gives a much better idea of what help is needed; that engaging personally with the situation creates a greater likelihood of sustained interest and commitment.

Jo and Ian Mintern

Jo and Ian had only been married six months and had never been to Africa! For them this was a real, shared adventure which took them way beyond their comfort zones! Jo works in the travel industry and Ian is a local bus driver.

Jo's reflection following the visit was that it is great to be part of the answer to the problems of Africa.

Ian reflected that it was beautiful to see God's love shared between His people, that it was very much a two-way exchange between nations. He really enjoyed seeing how the money that is sent is used, how it is changing people's lives and seeing the children growing up in secure Christian environments.

As a couple they lost the wallet which contained most of their money for the duration of the trip. It had been hidden in some work boots, which then had been given away! Naturally they were upset and concerned. The team prayed! The person who had been given the boots was found and the wallet was still there with all the money still in it. In the face of poverty the money could so easily have been taken; it was, after all, a fortune in comparison to what the person had day by day. But integrity amongst Ugandan Christians is high, and the money was fully returned. This experience was powerful for Ian and Jo and the rest of the team.

Ian's final reflections was that he loved being in a situation where there were so few distractions —our life in the West is so full of them and he longs to lead a more focussed life.

Reflections from some of the Teenagers:
Matt De Silva / James Trevithick
Arran McDougall / Katie Trevithick

- Good to experience a different culture
- Out of our comfort zone is stretching and good
- Great to see a totally different way of life
- Great to see firsthand what we have only seen on TV
- Enjoyed getting my hands dirty – really getting involved
- Watched films on the way out but on the way back home I just want to make a difference in life and do something
- It makes you appreciate things more
- It seemed daunting at first but it's been better than I could ever imagine
- It's been great to have teenagers working alongside us teenagers

Carlos Clarke

Carlos has been on three Watoto teams, and this time he took on leadership responsibility. Carlos is a Community Support Officer.

Carlos reckons that it's one thing giving to a project, but by engaging with it means you put your heart into it – that means you take it into the long term of life. If your heart's in it then you take that home with you and want to remain involved.

He thinks observation is one thing but participation is to be part of the vision. He believes these visits are about practical and spiritual vision being moulded together. Building classrooms and encouraging one another spiritually work well together.

He says that if he goes back it will always be more to do with relationships than the build project itself – even though he sees the buildings as crucial.

Carlos has learnt through these visits that we are part of a much bigger work of God that goes on around the whole world. He sees it as a great privilege to be part of God's family united together despite geographical distance.

Norman Head

Norman has travelled a great deal in Africa and is an actuary in the City of London. He feared that in some way the team might be patronising for differing reasons yet found that this was not the case at all.

Norman enjoyed realising that without us being there the Ugandan builders would not have employment and the buildings might never have been funded (the teams raise that capital); he also noted that the relationship between them and the team was truly amazing.

Norman was really blessed by Jackson, the Ugandan foreman, who was so calm, wise, gracious and prayerful. He would always start the day with devotions, which would include everyone, and he was never fazed by whatever pressures came his way.

Pam Jardine

Pam had not been to Africa before, and in England she is a Practice Nurse. She is glad for short visits like this because it means you don't have to give up your job to go.

Other benefits for her were getting closer to God and a new perspective on her life as a whole; she has become more involved in the local church, and it has enabled her to realise that she can make a difference using her skills abroad.

Pam pointed out that the whole experience was not just the two weeks going to Gulu but the eighteen month run-up in terms of training, team building and fundraising which were all part of the experience.

Action

1. Create a list of what stood out for you from what the team have said.

> 1)
>
> 2)
>
> 3)
>
> 4)
>
> 5)
>
> 6)
>
> 7)
>
> 8)

2. Get together with a friend or home group and discuss together those 'stand out' points.

17

Mission in the DNA of Church Life

Having a vicar who is essentially an evangelist does not necessarily make parochial life that easy! Ask my church! But it does mean that everything in church life has a mission edge to it. We exist as Christians in order to reach the lost. The church exists for mission. We are not here just to bless the found but are here to search out the lost.

We are a mission church, not a church that does mission.

Jesus told three stories in a row to emphasise to us that mission needs to be the priority: the lost coin, the lost sheep and the lost son. Jesus came to seek and save the lost. In the focussed way he lived he did upset the religious who were far more inwardly-looking. We desperately need to re-establish in today's church that emphasis of reaching out to the majority who know nothing of what it means to know Christ.

We planted St Saviour's Church, Sunbury, in 2002 with thirty-seven adults and approximately twenty children. We are now over three hundred of all ages, and our greatest growth area is young families. On Easter morning this year of 2012 we baptised by full immersion fourteen people who have decided to follow Jesus. It is the most wonderful celebration when people proclaim faith and are baptised. It is also incredibly evangelistic.

Over the years, we as a church have had all kinds of things levelled against us, such as we only grow through transferred growth (Christians church-hopping). Why Christians waste so much time criticising each other when there is the massive job of evangelism to be done, I don't know. But what I do know is that since we came to Sunbury we have seen people consistently coming into relationship with Jesus, be baptised and start their discipleship journey. The discipleship course we are running these days is fantastic, put together by Rev. Paul Oxley, one of my brilliant curates. He has called it 'Foundations' and is worthy of being published in its own right. It is levelled for people just taking off, those like me in mid-flight and those who have been flying forever!

From the start of our church there was mission in its DNA. Church planting has always been talked about as a goal, and we have with us a pioneer called Rev. Tim Rose, who will lead our fist team off as soon as the Bishop has created an opening for us. My other curate, Rev. Paul Oxley, has just launched St Mark's MK (www.stmarksmk.com). This is a brand new Anglican planting initiative in one of the fastest growing cities in Europe. These are exciting days and we are seeing the local church grow. Our vision is to see the local church grow through living faith, authentic worship and practical love.

It is my experience that church members who come with me on short-term mission visits return home with an increased living faith, a life that is centred on worshipping God and a huge desire to reach out in practical love. So, for me as a church leader, the opportunity for people to go is vital.

Team members often return home with the priority of mission being much higher on their agenda than when they left. This sense of urgency, this enthusiasm and fire for mission, is what is often sadly lacking in the Western Church.

The fire of mission has gone out so much in the Western Church that universalism has crept quietly through the back door of many churches, ensuring that the church remains evangelistically inactive and in certain decline.

Action

1. Discuss with a friend or your home group what priority you think mission should have in the Christian's and local church's life.

2. Discuss with friends or as a home group what universalism is and how much it is affecting our attitude towards mission.

18

Who Could I Go on Such a Visit With?

Mission Organisations/Practical Tips

It is possible for you to go, and the following mission organisations certainly organise visits:

- **Watoto**
  Global Teams to Uganda / Visit Africa Office:
  Email: *europe@watoto.com*

- **Interserve**
  On Track Teams to Asia:
  Email: *info@interserve.org.uk*

- **Tearfund**
  Transform Teams
  Email: *enquiry@tearfund.org*

- **Church Missionary Society**
  Short Term Encounter Teams
  Email: *teams@cms-uk.org*

- SOMA – Sharing of Ministries Abroad
  (Anglican Short Term Mission Agency)
  International Teams
  Email: *somauknd@btinternet.com*

- MAF (Mission Aviation Fellowship)
  Internal Flights – getting teams to difficult places
  Website: *www.maf-uk.org*

Over twenty-five years I have had the privilege of taking many thousands of people on teams.

If you would like to go on a very practical visit which might do one of the following things:

- Build a house/classroom for orphaned African children
- Assist with children's holiday clubs
- Work alongside abused women

...then **Watoto** has a lot to offer in terms of opportunity.

If you are looking to be involved with a more spiritually-inclined programme, then a **SOMA** team might well be more appropriate.

Interserve, **CMS** and **Tearfund** have all kinds of teams with all sorts of opportunities – do look at their websites or, even better, ring their offices to find out more.

You will never regret *going* and you most certainly will *grow*.

19

Debriefing When You Come Back

Over the years I have found that the people who get the most out of these experiences are those who give themselves time to reflect. It is also important to debrief on your return so that you can acclimatise back into your culture. Some people, as I have done, do experience culture shock and this can be quite disorientating.

Debriefing involves going over a number of points that will allow you to reflect on your time away. It is also very helpful to talk things over with someone, especially if you have been to an area like Congo, where much trauma has been witnessed.

As part of your debriefing you can make some assessments of your effectiveness during that time and can identify both the things you think you did right and the things that you think you were not so happy about! It is also a time for sharing any insights you may have gained that will help other team members in the years to come. Debriefing is a vital part of the closure process.

As part of your debrief, set aside a time for reflection on the following Bible passage:

Philippians 4:8-9:

Finally, brothers, whatever is true, whatever is noble, whatever is right, whatever is pure, whatever is lovely, whatever is admirable – think about such things. Whatever you have learned or received from me, or seen in me – put it into practice. And the God of peace will be with you.

Using this verse as a springboard, spend an hour or so alone, reflecting on your mission's experience. As you reflect, make a list of the things you are grateful to God for during your time on the visit. List them under the headings of true, noble, pure, lovely and admirable.

In your notebook, record the following:

- What you have learnt through your experience?
- What you have received from God through it?
- What you have seen in the lives of your fellow workers that you would like to incorporate into your life?
- What you have seen God do in the lives of the people with whom you have ministered?
- Pray and ask God to show you how you can work these new insights and values into your life once you are back home. Record the specific insights He shows you.
- List the obstacles that might prevent you from incorporating these new values and insights into your life. Pray about strategies to overcome them.
- Are there any suggestions you would like to make with regard to improving the preparation or leadership of the mission?
- Finally, write yourself a letter. Pretend you are writing to a friend, and include in it the most important points you have covered in your personal debriefing. Put the letter in an envelope and address it to your home address.

Ask a reliable friend/leader to mail the letter to you in five or six months' time. When it arrives, it will be a surprise and a great encouragement to you. You will also be able to measure how well you are doing in applying to your life at home all the things you learned on the visit. Agree with yourself that when you receive the letter, you will correct any deviation that may have crept in from the course you set for your life.

Recommended Reading

Author's Recommendation

Re-Entry   by Peter Jordan
                              Published by Youth With a Mission

Related Books from Onwards and Upwards Publishers

Building Hope   by Bryan Parr
The autobiography of a man who simply asked God, "Is this all there is to the Christian life?" and then began the most unexpected adventure, discovering how God could use his practical building skills on short-term missions to bring hope to the most needy of Eastern Europeans.

Below Me, the Clouds   by Ron Collard
The remarkable experiences of a former MAF pilot.

Where Love Leads You   by Ruth Stranex Deeth
The tale of an ordinary woman who simply gave her life into the hands of God and served on the African mission field. God's miraculous provision and protection unfold in the most extraordinary ways.

Tracing the Golden Thread   by Mary Weeks Millard
The life story of a nurse who served as a missionary in East and Central Africa and saw how God could take a simple skill and use it to transform communities.

Diamonds in the Darkness   by Pat Marsh
The story of a remarkable woman who made herself available to God wherever she went. Her writings provide inspiration for anyone engaged in community health or those listening for an authentic voice of contemporary Christian mission.